The Inside, the Downside, the Up-side, the Funny Side of Comedy's Sensational New Superstar
ELLEN DeGENERES

Why did Ellen travel the country in a Winnebago with a big nose on the front?

What was historic about her appearance on the *Tonight Show?*

How did *The Wonder Years* lead to the creation of her sitcom *Ellen?*

What were the two *flop* sitcoms on which Ellen costarred previously?

What sitcom was she supposed to do . . . and why is she glad she didn't?

What two movies did Ellen make?

What is her beverage of choice?

When and why did Ellen first tell jokes?

What's the surprising connection between Ellen and *Saturday Night Live*'s "Mr. Bill Show"?

Find Out All About the New Queen of Comedy in

ELLEN DeGENERES UP CLOSE!

Ellen DeGeneres
UP CLOSE

The Unauthorized Biography of the
Hot New Star of
ABC's
ELLEN

KATHY TRACY and JEFF ROVIN

POCKET BOOKS

New York   London   Toronto   Sydney   Tokyo   Singapore

An *Original* Publication of POCKET BOOKS

 POCKET BOOKS, a division of Simon & Schuster Inc.
1230 Avenue of the Americas, New York, NY 10020

ISBN: 0-671-51734-1

First Pocket Books printing October 1994

10 9 8 7 6 5 4 3 2 1

POCKET and colophon are registered trademarks of Simon & Schuster Inc.

Cover photo © Roger Karnbad/Michelson

Printed in the U.S.A.

Acknowledgments

Though there are only three names on the cover of this book (and though Ellen may have *lived* her life, she didn't contribute to this unauthorized biography), many talented people helped the authors put it together.

To begin with, there were dozens of people at ABC, at Sony Pictures Studio, at Touchstone Television, and other sources around Hollywood who contributed information and observations.

They know who they are, and we thank them.

The staffs of the *Citizens Journal* and the Chamber of Commerce in Atlanta, Texas, were not only helpful but extremely courteous, as were the students and faculty of Ellen's schools, several of whom wished to remain anonymous. Their reminiscences were invaluable.

Many people in New Orleans, who also wish to

go unnamed, recounted memories and provided information to this biography. Several DeGeneres family members gave us insights into Ellen's life and comedy routines.

We've spoken with a number of stand-ups and actors, and we'd especially like to thank those who are quoted herein.

This book also could not have been written without help from Stephen, David, and especially Barry and Judy.

We would also like to thank Ellen DeGeneres. Though we didn't get to talk to her on the record for this book, she is one of those celebrities—one of an increasingly rare breed—who doesn't shut herself off from the press or place stultifying pre-conditions on interviews. She understands that even successful shows need to be talked up in the press; that successful stars need to keep lines of communication open with their fans in order to *stay* successful; and that you either control your press or it controls you.

She's as smart as she is funny, and we hope our admiration for her is evident in these pages.

Introduction

One of the earliest gags Ellen DeGeneres wrote for her stand-up routine went like this:

> You ever notice whenever you're with someone and they taste something that tastes bad, they always want you to taste it immediately.
> "This is dis*gus*ting. Taste it."

Though she didn't realize it at the time, this would become an appropriate metaphor for life in the limelight.

More often than not, biographies and autobiographies are like that. This is especially true today, when tabloid TV shows compete—all with open checkbooks—for the daily dirt. In order to stand out, print has got to sizzle. Or reek, depending on your point of view.

As a result, writers and reporters chronicle lives that taste pretty bad in spots—sometimes awfully bad in a great *many* spots—and then ask the reader or viewer to taste it. What's amazing is that, rubberneckers and voyeurs that we are, we do just that. And the worse it is, the more we consume.

Comedian Sandra Bernhart was signing her semi-autobiographical *Love, Love, and Love* at a bookstore recently in Studio City, California.

Looking up at one eager fan, Sandra said, "I bet you're not even going to wait to get home to start reading. I can tell. You're the type who *loves* this."

She was teasing, of course, but the fan said she was absolutely right: He'd been flipping through the book while in line, looking to see if there was anything about Sandra's highly publicized friendship with Madonna.

Taste it. . . .

Our appetite for personal details of the stars is insatiable, and the seamier those details are, the better we like them.

Joan Collins's *Past Imperfect* reads like one of her sister Jackie's novels; Roseanne Arnold's second book of memoirs, *My Life,* was so sensational that the media had played out its best parts before the autobiography even hit the bookshelves; and Barry Williams's otherwise innocuous *Growing Up Brady* seems to have been a bestseller mostly because of the author's revelations about a lustful relationship with TV mom Florence Henderson. (At a party celebrating ABC's fortieth anniversary, the enticing Ms. Henderson commented, "It's like a forest fire—isn't it?—this process of disseminating personal details. You wouldn't think a spark so small could be fanned into something that consumes so very many trees.")

Aspects of Ellen's life have taken on many of the "taste-me" trappings, and though her life experiences aren't quite in a league with those of Liz and the late Jackie O. (or Roseanne, it seems), Ellen's had a fair share of hardship and tragedy in her nearly thirty-seven years. What's more, since the debut of her half-hour sitcom, *These Friends of Mine,* in March of 1994, there have been dramatic and unexpected conflicts, controversies, and compromises.

The biggest adjustment she's had to make is the fact that her formerly private life, which might seem eccentric to a large section of her TV audience, has suddenly become fodder for the tabloid press.

Onstage, Ellen has always been an observer of life and relationships, but in all her routines she tells us about *us*—rarely about herself. Most of her "autobiographical" stories are generic enough that everyone can relate to them.

That she may have to make changes in the way she lives her own life has certainly put a bad taste in *her* mouth. In the pre-sitcom days, living in San Francisco and then in Los Angeles, Ellen always came and went as she pleased and enjoyed relative anonymity. Now, she says, that's impossible. Fans stop and ask for her autograph, something that's "starting to happen more and more since the show's been on the air." Even now, after several months of this, "when it does happen, it catches me off-guard."

Ellen doesn't resent the attention, of course. To the contrary. She says that before the show, reruns of her stand-up act on HBO and excerpts on shows like *Stand-Up, Stand-Up* and *Short Attention Span Theater* on cable's Comedy Central are what "kept my career going." That's not quite true, but it is true that some thirty million people who didn't know her in February know her now.

And while she's never asked for it, Ellen has another problem—or responsibility, depending on how you look at it: She's become a standard-bearer for young single women. Blue-collar homemakers have had tough and resilient Roseanne as a role model and spokesperson for six years (yes, it *does* seem longer); career-oriented women have had Murphy Brown to look up to; and hard-working single mothers have embraced sarcastic, determined Brett Butler.

But until Ellen came along, no one on prime-time television spoke for relatively sane, single, baby boomer, non-superachievers. While Ellen Morgan is essentially a Greek chorus for other peoples' relationships, her character is very specifically defined: She's obviously man-free and not at all uncomfortable to be so. That's a baton she'd never expected to be carrying, and now that she has it it'll be fascinating to see where she runs with it.

* * *

How much of that standard-bearer is Ellen DeGeneres, and how much of that is her TV character, Ellen Morgan?

Suffice it to say, for now, that she's finding it a remarkably comfortable fit. And that's good, because she's looking at what will probably be a six- or seven-year hitch on prime-time TV.

Ellen has a good idea of what the immediate future holds for the fictional Ellen (change is in the cards), but what about the years ahead for the real one? The show will shut down every year from March through August, and though Ellen will have to be available in early July to supervise scripts for the coming season, that leaves plenty of time for other activities.

Are there more movies in her future? (There have already been two not-terribly successful movies in her past).

Will she return regularly to the stand-up stage? And if she does, what will audiences think when they get DeGeneres instead of Morgan? (Fellow comic Tim Allen, star of *Home Improvement,* has had a real problem with that. "It's difficult for me to tone my act down so that children won't be offended," he confides. "My stand-up's been ravaged by this. When I tone it down, it doesn't have the same rock 'n' roll feeling, and I don't enjoy it as much. But when I look out at these nine- and twelve-year-old faces, what am I gonna do? I don't want them asking after the show, 'Mama, what's a blowjob?' I have more responsibility now, whether I asked for it or not.")

And what about the Ellen of Christmas Past? What were the events that shaped her life and humor? Is she "on" offstage or, like so many stand-ups, is she brooding and shy and strangely unfunny when she's away from the spotlight?

Who are her friends, what does she think of other comedians (in particular, the rival she never asked for, Jerry Seinfeld), and what is it about the lifestyle of the suddenly rich and famous Ellen that makes her so controversial?

Taste it—it's fascinating!

Ellen DeGeneres
UP CLOSE

1

Ellen . . . Then

*A professional is someone who does their best
even when they don't feel like it.*

—Charlton Heston

Shortly after she'd won Showtime's "Funniest Person in America" competition, Ellen agreed to do a gig for some three hundred Marines.

Male Marines. Not a woman among them.

No big deal, she thought. They were people with funny bones, as susceptible to a good joke as the next person. They'd been laughing at Bob Hope for years. Of course, Bob Hope always warmed them up with the likes of Ann-Margret and Loni Anderson.

Typically, a stand-up's agent will make sure that the fit of comic and audience is a good one. They'll try not to book hydrophobics on a cruise ship or off-color comics on Nickelodeon—that sort of thing.

But Ellen didn't have an agent back then, someone to tell her that she and the military might not be a good mix, that her extensive life experiences might not match those of very many soldiers, that the few and the proud would not necessarily be the attentive and the polite.

At the time, the centerpiece of Ellen's act was her moving "Phone Call to God" routine, in which she puts in a plaintive call to heaven to ask, among other things, why fleas are alive. The monologue was inspired by a genuine loss in Ellen's life, and it's one of her best and most personal routines.

Ellen took to the stage after a very popular, very loud, very macho comedian had whipped the crowd into a testosterone frenzy. The front row was acting particularly randy and, short of Madonna, no one was going to win points with them.

"Let's hear it for the *Funniest Person in America!*" the host whooped as he motioned for Ellen to come out to sparse applause—and to the slaughter. He smiled and winked at the slender, blond twenty-four-year-old as she approached, and then he glanced toward the audience and gave them a thumbs-up as he walked offstage.

Having been standing in the wings, Ellen knew only too well what the crowd was in the mood for. They wanted more of the host's childishness and misogyny, buckets of it, and not a "Phone Call to God." But there was absolutely nothing she could do about it.

Watching her take that long walk onstage, one of the other entertainers on the bill remembers thinking that he wished he'd brought a cartload of pies and a Fang puppet to hand to Ellen as she walked out. A Soupy Sales routine would've played just fine here. But he didn't, and stand-ups are like human cannonballs: Once they're in the barrel, they're going for the ride.

Ellen had faced tough audiences before, and she told herself she'd get through this. Besides, if she walked off the stage it would seriously damage her career and embarrass Showtime. Comedy club owners and booking agents don't care what your reasons might be: If you walk away from a gig, you aren't going to get another.

There were scattered catcalls when Ellen stepped behind the microphone. But she could deal with that. What really threw her was when she started her set and several of the revved-up boys in the front row actually stood, turned their chairs around, and faced the back of the room. A couple of them began talking among themselves, and a few even yelled to other members of the audience, who yelled back. None of the other Marines had the courtesy or courage to ask for quiet, and Ellen was smart enough not to engage the hecklers in a debate. They'd have eaten her alive.

Unarmed and alone, Ellen stormed the beach, hoping that enough of the audience would let themselves get hooked by the material to keep her afloat.

They didn't.

She tried not to become disconnected from the material; if it became rote, just words, it would be even worse for her. It wasn't the same as bombing, which, like all comedians, Ellen had done on a number of occasions. It's hell, of course. When you bomb, time crawls by, your mouth grows dry while your palms grow moist, and there's a still and deadly silence in the audience, like the quiet after a car crash. But it's feedback, part of the comedy process, and at least the reaction isn't personal.

This was.

It was a rejection of Ellen because she was a woman, because she wasn't part of the rude boys' club, and she'd never experienced anything like *that* before.

Many comedians have a safety valve when they bomb. They realize that the audience has tensed up in empathy, so they try to relax them by "calling" what's happening: admitting that they're dying and trying to turn it into a joke.

"Hey, this isn't working, is it? What happened— you all come in here just to hide from the cops? You see an old lover comin' and decided this'd be a good time to check into the darkest spot you could find?"

But Ellen was beyond calling, beyond trying to win over the audience. She was determined to get through the material for her own self-respect.

She stopped doing the routine for the audience and did it for herself—and for the lost friend for whom the centerpiece was written.

The minutes dragged by.

When her set was finally finished and Ellen walked offstage, she passed the male comedian. They didn't make eye contact as he headed back to the stage.

The audience cheered his return, their applause

and foot-stomping way out of proportion with his reappearance. It continued as he held up his hands, like Mark Antony preparing to address the citizens of Rome.

"How about *that!*" he yelled to his followers.

There were mock cheers and a few boos. But he wasn't quite through with Ellen.

"Let's hear it one more time for"—he paused after each word to make sure they hurt—"the . . . *Funniest . . . Person . . . in . . . AMERICA!*"

By this time Ellen was walking slowly through the darkness of the wings, her face downturned. She was angry, not humiliated, and she just wanted to get away. Part of her wanted to drive nonstop to Tyler, Texas, throw herself into her mother's arms, and forget for a moment the cruelty of show business. But that was not the part of Ellen that was calling the shots.

Ellen had been in the business for a little over a year and she had discovered, very early in her young career, that there was nothing to compare with a group of people laughing at something she had written in the privacy of her own apartment or in her Winnebago or in a bar. In fact, if anything, her performance here tonight had underscored one thing: how very much she loved stand-up. Otherwise there was no way she'd stay in it a minute longer.

Underneath her open, very vulnerable surface, Ellen was still finding that she had a lot of steel in her. And just as she had when overcoming personal or professional crises in the past, she waited until she got back to her hotel room and wrote down what she was feeling, looked for the truth and humor in what had happened.

The next morning, though the rejection still stung, an observation made by Charlotte Whitton pretty much summed up the way Ellen felt.

"Whatever women do they must do twice as well as men to be thought half as good. Luckily, this is not difficult."

2
Ellen . . . Now

A star is someone who, when an audience approves of them, puts more into what they're doing, not less.

—Elvis Presley

Over a decade later, early in 1994, a smiling, buoyant Ellen DeGeneres is showing television reporters around the set of her new show at Sony Pictures Studio in Culver City.

Formerly the Metro-Goldwyn-Mayer Studios, home of Elizabeth Taylor and Gene Kelly, Mickey Rooney and Judy Garland, Fred Astaire and *Gone With the Wind,* the lot was for a few brief months in the spring of 1994 best known as the Domain of DeGeneres, the star of the half-hour sitcom called *These Friends of Mine.* (The show has since moved to the Disney Studios; more on this later on.)

One of the crewmen, a crusty old-timer standing by a doughnut and coffee cart, tells a reporter, "We've got a street named after Stallone here, which seems a little ridiculous [the *Rocky* films were shot on the lot], but at least he's in movies. If you'd told someone back in the 1950s that the biggest shot at the studio would be a comedian who's got a television show and dresses in sneakers, jeans, and sweatshirts, no one would've believed it."

"Shit," says another crewman, standing nearby, "Lucille Ball had to build her own studio [Desilu] to get things done the way she wanted." He laughs. "And even then, her name came second, after Desi's."

True.

But times have changed, and more people see Ellen DeGeneres every week than saw Liz or Judy or even Sly in any of their movies.

There are several "standing sets" for the show—sets that are not taken down at any time during the season while the show is in production. (After the season, the props are carefully stored, the flats that comprise the walls are knocked down and stacked, and the soundstage is used to shoot motion pictures.)

Ellen walks through the apartment set, with its living-room/kitchen combination—a configuration that's been seen on *Designing Women, Home Improvement,* and countless other shows. Set designers use this setup because it allows characters to move around, cut up veggies, or pour themselves orange juice while they talk, which keeps scenes from becoming too static. Ellen is particularly pleased with the apartment set because, as she tells one reporter, a faint Louisiana twang in her voice, "People love to see puppies and kids, so I have photos of them all around my apartment."

As is usual for TV, the different sets have been constructed wall-to-wall in a row. This saves space as well as time, since the big cameras can simply be rolled to the left or right when the scene changes. In addition to Ellen's apartment, the other standing sets include the Buy the Book bookstore/café where she works, with its adjoining office for grumpy boss Susan.

These sets have been erected in front of a long, stadiumlike grandstand from which an audience of some two hundred guests can watch the filming. Tickets to the grandstand are free; after the debut, however, they've been extremely difficult to obtain. Even network VIPs and friends of the cast, crew, and producers, who are accustomed to sitting in the front row, have a tough time getting seats *anywhere*.

The sets are built beneath clustered banks of lights that make Ellen Morgan's world unnaturally bright in person. It has to be this way, however, since a great deal of light is lost in the electronics of putting the show on film.

Between the sets and the peanut gallery there's just enough room for the three cameras that tape the show from different angles, a red light on top of each telling the performers which one is filming at any given time. Large television monitors hang in front of the grandstand so that whenever the cameras get in the way, the audience can watch what's being taped. Curiously, even when their view of the set is unobstructed, many people tend to watch the monitors. Habit, one supposes.

Behind the set is the green room, where stars and their guests can relax and have a quick meal. For Ellen, that means a salad—no croutons—and an ice tea or water. From time to time she has one of the Very Fine Juices, a beverage she plugs in ads. A bottle of water may actually be "lunch": Ellen's culinary habits are so Spartan that, watching her, one frequently wonders where she gets all of her energy. (A staffer says, "She seems to store it. She'll be real quiet for a while, then get incredibly active, revving from zero to sixty in a heartbeat. It's amazing the way she does that.")

The green room is pretty much the only place where the stars of the show *do* socialize. In Hollywood, actors rarely get together away from the studio. Not only have they had enough of each other after twelve-plus-hour days but, as Pat Richardson of *Home Improvement* puts it, "A successful show is like a marriage: You'll be working together for many, many years, so you have to treat your relationship with respect and caution. You don't want to find out if the old saying about familiarity breeding contempt is true. The worst thing that can happen is that you start hating one another for some reason. You just don't want to risk blowing the chemistry you have."

Near the green room is a makeup area. The makeup chair is one of Ellen's least-favorite places to be. Ellen never wears makeup off-camera. As she once said in her act, the reason is that she "was raised by the wolves. All male wolves. They didn't wear makeup, although one did wear deodorant, so I learned about that. So that's good." She adds, "But the one bad thing is that whenever I see a gazelle, my mouth waters, and I get the urge to chase it."

Ellen seems to subscribe wholeheartedly to the idea put forth by fellow comedian Cathy Ladman that "makeup is such a weird concept. I'll wake up in the morning and look in the mirror: 'Gee, I really don't look so good. Maybe if my eyelids were blue, I'd be more attractive. . . .'"

Yet Ellen insists—rather incredibly—"I really don't like the way I look." She can't decide what bugs her more: the shape of her nose or her hangdog eyes or her round-shouldered posture. She feels that her features are "too rubberized." Like most of us, she's way too hard on herself. Naturally rosy-cheeked, with big, arresting eyes—what *The New York Times* described as "large round periwinkle eyes"—she's attractive and seems to personify the no-nonsense, no-gloss young woman of the Clinton era. She's also somewhat more slender than she looks on TV. For various and complex reasons, television cameras seem to add about ten pounds to people (which inspired TV personality Kitty Carlisle to quip, "So I make it a policy never to eat TV cameras").

A short walk from the set is Ellen's dressing room. It has to be nearby because there isn't a lot of time between scenes for the star to return phone calls or just plain relax. Also, Ellen needs a private place she can go to quickly to memorize the fifty-plus-page scripts. Or to learn the twenty to thirty pages of rewrites that come in once they start rehearsing and see what plays well and what doesn't. Unfortunately, there isn't enough room in here for exercise equipment. At home, Ellen stays fit and clears her head by working out several hours every day on a NordicTrack or a LifeCycle, lifting weights, or doing aerobics and situps.

Leading the reporters toward her dressing room, Ellen moves confidently, with big, easy strides, her eyes constantly on the move. It comes as no surprise when she reveals that she once considered being a professional athlete. All right, it was just golf, but she also played a lot of tennis when she was younger, and she does carry herself with that Nancy Lopez–Billie Jean King kind of authority.

What's great for visitors to the set, especially members of the press, network executives, or advertising reps, is that Ellen tends to be "on" with them: If something funny occurs to her, she'll say it; if it gets a laugh, she'll remember it. Noisy pipes here at the erstwhile home of MGM might cause her to wonder if Esther Williams is lost; a technical glitch may inspire her to call out, *"HAL . . . HAL, is that you?"*

Ellen's humor can be subtle and oblique like that, but it can also be delightfully over-the-top.

On the very first day of taping her series, the daily syndicated show *Entertainment Tonight* has come to the set to cover the stand-up's activities.

The show has followed Ellen around before, when she was on the comedy-club circuit, only she isn't *quite* as laid back now as she was then.

She's juiced, in fact.

Ellen introduces her attractive, silver-haired mother Betty to the *ET* crew and gives her a peck on the lips. The ultrasupportive Betty is more important to Ellen than anyone on the planet.

"Should people watch the show, or what?" Ellen asks her mother.

"Oh, puh-*lease!*" Betty implores, facing the camera like a pro and flashing a big, proud smile. "You won't want to miss it. . . . It's going to be so funny! It's wonderful . . . just great."

"That's right," Ellen says, then looks from her mother to the camera. With seasoned comic timing, she deadpans, "She wants a condo."

Before going to her dressing room, Ellen pops outside the soundstage to show *Entertainment Tonight* what she considers one of the greatest perks of her blossoming stardom: the brand-new golf cart she's been given for getting around the lot in a hurry.

"That's what they give you when you have your own TV show," she says, and she's not kidding: Things like this are typically written into stars' contracts these days. It wouldn't do for a star to have to walk a couple of hundred yards to their cars or trailers.

Naturally, for the benefit of *Entertainment Tonight,* the cart goes out of control and carries Ellen off on a Pee-wee-esque adventure.

When she finally reaches her dressing room, she proudly displays the door, which is adorned with ELLEN in bold letters; beneath it, instead of the traditional star, there's a sunflower decal. It's an appropriate symbol for the blond young star who really comes to life under the spotlight.

The dimly lit dressing room is modest. The dressing rooms of most TV stars are rarely more than that. Unlike movie stars, who may want to sleep at the studios to hide from the press (or carry on with costars), who have to wait around for hours while sets are lit and camera angles chosen using stand-ins, TV actors don't spend a great deal of time in their dressing rooms.

The walls of Ellen's room are drab yellow; a big white sofa is set against one of them, with a wooden chair to the right. There's a small lacquered table in front of it, a dresser on the opposite wall, a tall lamp tucked in a corner, and, attached to the wall, a sprawling lighting fixture that looks like metal pretzels laid end-to-end.

The camera catches glimpses of pinup posters of *Entertainment Tonight* hosts Mary Hart, John Tesh, and Leeza Gibbons. Ellen didn't have a poster of the show's respected film commentator Leonard Maltin, so she drew his portrait in magic marker and tacked it up behind the door. She apologizes: "Y'know, I'm not completely sure that he has this gap here *[in his beard],* so I've gotta fill it in some more."

Tesh's compact disc *A Romantic Christmas* lies beside the CD player ("It's a sexy CD," Ellen gushes); on the small table by the sofa is a dog-eared copy of Leonard Maltin's *Movie and Video Guide 1994;* and the top of a dresser has been transformed into a shrine, with low, burning candles sitting before framed photos of the hosts.

Ellen also assures viewers that she's wearing *Entertainment Tonight* underwear.

Ellen kneels before the shrine, shuts her eyes, folds her hands, and says a silent prayer to the *Entertainment Tonight* gods, hoping that her show will be a success. She's learned how to play the game, albeit in what can only be described as "DeGenerese": Through her utter sincerity, she tweaks the absurdity of this necessary press court-ship without demeaning it—or herself. (Unfortunately, Ellen will soon learn that her disarming manner isn't nearly enough to deflect the hungry eye of the tabloid press, which will be drawn to the decidedly nonmainstream aspects of her private life.)

For now, though, still using DeGenerese, the comedian skillfully deflects the kinds of compari-sons that can only lead to disappointment.

When one of the *Entertainment Tonight* report-ers mentions to Ellen that her show is being com-pared with *Seinfeld,* something that privately rankles the comedian—her stand-up routines have always, and inaccurately, been compared with his —she admits with a shrug, "It's more *Seinfeld* than it is *Bonanza."*

Later, when the same reporter points out that Ellen is also being called the Mary Tyler Moore of the nineties, she responds to the flattering but very premature remark by stating that she's actually "the female Shaquille O'Neal."

The taping of the first show goes extremely well, lasting just about three hours for the half-hour show. (That's not bad at all: Some shows run four hours or more, not just because of flubbed lines, but also costume changes, moving the cameras to other sets, and lighting those sets. Rewrites also go on through the taping process, when lines fall flat with the audience. Some shows also have to do "pick-ups," scenes that didn't work the previous week and required extensive retooling.)

When the evening's work is finished, there are congratulations all around, the cast and crew wishing each other a good weekend. Everyone will be back at work on Monday for the read-through of the next episode.

Ellen and her mother skip the golf cart and walk to the car, the thirty-six-year-old comedian feeling good about the show. More important, Ellen feels very good about where she is in her life. That terrible night with the Marines seems as though it happened to someone else. Someone who learned that, while comedy springs from adversity, so does strength.

Ellen has gone from being hooted to being feted. And now, instead of wanting to run home to her mother, Ellen is taking her mother home. Because Ellen was only kidding: Betty already has that condo in West Hollywood, not far from where Ellen herself lives up in the Hollywood Hills with a pair of cats, two "mean, mean dogs, and a pool and all the trappings." (Ellen jokes that her entire family "smelled the money and moved right out.")

All the hardship and suffering is finally paying off.

Whether it's because of Ellen's mock prayer in her dressing room, her mother's overt campaigning, heavy promotion from ABC, Ellen's wonderful TV persona, or all of the above (well, at least the last two, anyway), people do watch the show when it airs. They watch in huge numbers, thirty million on the average.

It's a weekly audience that dwarfs those to which her loud, very macho San Francisco nemesis played to in his entire career *combined.* Numbers that are larger than all but a handful of other shows on television.

Ellen has certainly benefited from the current trend of giving just about every successful stand-up comic from Roseanne Arnold to Paul Reiser her or his own situation comedy. However, if she didn't have qualities that struck a chord with the viewing public, she'd have been gone faster than you can say "Paula Poundstone."

Critics and industry observers are divided about the source of her appeal, as well as that of the show.

TV Guide calls Ellen "incredibly engaging," and

describes the show itself as a wonderful view of "those small moments that can make life such a pain."

Esquire thinks the heart of her appeal "is a sweetly expressed mistrust of everything," but attributes at least part of the show's success to being "inserted in the we-really-believe-in-you-so-you-better-not-screw-up slot after *Home Improvement.*"

Ellen herself feels the show is a hit because it appeals to "my gardener. He likes it. He doesn't speak English too well, but he thinks I make funny faces. At least I think that's what he said."

Well, the first two reviews are valid, anyway.

Whatever the reasons, *Ellen* (as her show is now called) is a smash, and so is Ellen DeGeneres. As is so often the case, it took her many years and a lot of hard work to become an overnight sensation.

3

I Only Laugh When It Hurts

When I was a girl I only had two friends, and they were imaginary. And they would only play with each other.

—Rita Rudner

In her act, Ellen says, "People always ask me, 'Were you funny as a child?'" Her answer: "Well, no. I was an accountant."

Odd as it may sound, Ellen *wasn't* funny as a child. Much later in her life, it was circumstances and her environment that made her so.

But then where Ellen comes from, people are accustomed to being affected by their surroundings. As people like playwright Tennessee Williams have observed, the relentlessly oppressive, steamy summer weather of the Deep South has a way of influencing personalities and shaping destinies. And for one with a restless soul, like Ellen, the very weight of the air can fuel dreams of escape.

* * *

Ellen DeGeneres was born on New Year's Day in 1958 and grew up in the Audubon Park section of New Orleans: a quiet, sleepy area five miles north of the historic French Quarter.

Unlike the Garden District with its striking antebellum-style homes and their sprawling grounds, Ellen's white-collar, middle-class neighborhood offered more modest dwellings built side-by-side in tight rows, many of them balanced on a foundation of neatly arranged cinder blocks. The yards were small, the streets were narrow, but the people were relaxed and friendly.

At the end of the long summer days, kids played outside until after dark, while their parents sat on the porch stoops, hoping for a moist breeze.

Ellen's father, soft-spoken Elliott DeGeneres, worked as an insurance salesman, while her mother, Betty Jane, took care of the house as well as Ellen and her brother, Vance, four years her senior.

Betty Jane Pfeffer had been married once before, to a young military man named George M. Simon. They'd been wed on February 11, 1950, and though they'd set up house in Baton Rouge, Simon himself lived on his out-of-state base.

That proved to be an unsatisfactory arrangement for them both. Apart more than they were together, the Simons separated after only eight months of marriage, and Betty moved to New Orleans.

After two years of separation—when Betty was comfortable that she wouldn't be an outcast by virtue of being a divorcée, and she was satisfied that she was making the right decision—the split was finalized.

Then as now, Betty was a fascinating, very creative, and fiercely independent woman. She's also full of love, which she very much needs to share. Thus in November of 1952, just one month after the divorce had finally become official, Betty tied the knot with Elliott DeGeneres, whom she had met in New Orleans.

Betty and Elliott come from large families, both of which had lived in the New Orleans/Baton Rouge area for several generations. The DeGeneres clan is especially well entrenched in the region and can trace its American roots to forefather John Constantine, an adventurous soul who, finding himself caught in a slave uprising on the French royal colony of St. Domaine in 1790, plotted to seek refuge in the newly independent United States.

With the help of a black nanny, Constantine snuck off the Caribbean island under cover of night and sailed to Alexandria, Virginia. Shortly after his arrival, he headed for southern Louisiana's thriving French enclave.

But while the current crop of Baton Rouge–based DeGenereses are a close-knit, very clannish group, Elliott and his kin have remained outsiders. This despite their geographical proximity to literally dozens of relatives.

The rest of the DeGenereses find this break

difficult to account for. Some family members believe that Betty was calling the shots and didn't really take to some of the yokels in the clan, while others say that she couldn't have been more person-able and sweet—not that the two are mutually exclusive. Still others maintain that the rather quiet, relatively conservative Elliott just didn't fit in with his rowdier kin.

In any event, says Kitty O'Neal, née DeGeneres, "Elliott's side of the family sort of drifted apart from the others. I don't remember ever seeing Elliott and his family at any gathering. We've thought of having a big family reunion to get all the DeGenereses together, which would be nice for Ellen.

"To be honest," Kitty adds, "I don't know how much, if at all, Ellen knows about her family's background. About a year ago, my son Peter went to see Ellen in concert, and afterward he went backstage and introduced himself. They talked for about an hour, and somehow Peter got on about our family tree.

"Well, Ellen was dumbfounded. She didn't have an inkling about any of her DeGeneres family history. She even called her father [who now lives in La Jolla, California] to ask if it were true. When he said he didn't know, she asked him to call *his* father. She really seemed fascinated.

"Ellen also admitted she knew nothing about the rest of the current family, and she seemed surprised and a bit taken aback by it all."

Another cousin, Kathy DeGeneres, says that

there's no bitterness at all about the estrangement, no sense that Ellen feels she's too good for the rest of the family.

To the contrary, "Everybody is thrilled for Ellen," she says. "Even if we don't know her personally, she's still family." However, Kathy does say that she was a little disappointed when, in March of 1994, several DeGenereses took the time to write to Ellen "in care of ABC to congratulate her [about her new show]. We never heard back."

(This doesn't mean that Ellen was ignoring them. Letters sent to the networks get forwarded, along with thousands of others, to publicists, managers, or production offices. Rarely do they reach the stars themselves.)

Cousin Buddy DeGeneres also says that he wishes Ellen were closer to the family because he thinks it would be a lot of fun to spend time with her. And while he agrees that the family is extremely happy for her, he says they've taken her achievements in stride.

"Talent runs in our family," he says matter-of-factly. "There are a lot of musicians among us. For example, my dad [Thomas] was in the group John Fred and His Playboy Band, which had the hit record "Judy in Disguise (With Glasses)" [in 1968].

"And everyone has a good sense of humor. You should hear the one-liners when we all get together. So it's no real surprise that someone from the family is a famous comedian."

Ellen is truly unaware of this untapped talent in her family, but Arsenio Hall was eerily on-target when he asked Ellen in 1989 if her newfound success had caused relatives she never heard of to come popping out of the woodwork?

She replied, "It's weird, yeah, that happens, y'know. People come up to me and—first of all, I have the worst memory anyway. So no matter who comes up to me they're just like, 'I can't believe you don't remember me.' 'I'm sorry—Oh . . . Dad.' I really don't. People come up to me. 'We were best friends! You don't remember?' And they tell me these wild things that we did. I don't even remember *having* a goat, first of all. I would remember that, I think. It happens all the time. So now I'm just, 'Oh sure, sure.' "

As a child, Ellen seldom stood out from the crowd. In fact, a woman who was her classmate at La Salle Elementary School remembers Ellen as being decidedly *un*remarkable.

"She wasn't a showoff or a class clown, or even all that funny," says the friend. "She was really just sort of average.

"La Salle was a small neighborhood school, the kind of place where everybody knew everybody. We'd go over to each other's house for birthday parties or to play, and Ellen's family was no different from the rest. There was nothing that made them stand out in your memory.

"That's why I was really surprised the first time I saw Ellen on TV. But the funniest thing is," says the friend, laughing, "she looks almost the same now as she did when we were in grade school. You look at her face and you still see the same little girl."

Even the way she walks and wears her hair is the same, says her friend.

At the time, Ellen had only one interest. She says, "I was obsessed with animals and I really thought I'd join the Peace Corps or go to Africa and study apes."

However, as she grew older and entered her teenage years, she admits that her little fantasy passed and, she says, "I had no idea what I wanted to do."

One problem Ellen had was that she lived in the shadow of her very outgoing brother. She usually surrendered conversation and center stage to him (along with most of the records she bought, remembers a friend of Vance's).

But that alone doesn't account for Ellen's quiet nature. She also worshiped her mother, and she wanted very much to be like her.

Slender, good-looking, and almost supernaturally poised, Betty was a model of composure and politeness. Meeting her then, one would understand how she didn't quite fit in with the rest of the boisterous, plain-speaking DeGeneres clan.

Ellen passionately admired her mother, and she tried very hard to emulate her. She wanted to know the big words, say the right things, not let things upset her—to be like her mother in every way. "The Little Lady," many of Ellen's schoolmates called her, and it was an apt description.

It was because of her extremely close relationship with her mother that Ellen first discovered her knack for comedy. As with many revelations, however, it came about as the result of a period of great trial for the family: When Ellen was thirteen, her parents separated.

None of the four members of the nuclear family has ever said what caused the breakup, though Betty appears to have a restless nature that may have contributed to the couple's problems. She's a very giving woman who has always liked being with a man, but she also dearly cherishes her independence. It would be inaccurate to say that she resented being a homemaker; she loved doing domestic chores, whether it was cleaning or knitting pairs of socks for her husband.

However, as a budding violinist and a fine dancer, she also had aspirations that went beyond being a wife and mother. She didn't know how to satisfy her ambition, but, this being the dawn of the age of women's liberation, she knew that she wasn't finding contentment where she was. She also doesn't appear to have been very happy with Elliott at this point, and she spent much time with her own small group of friends.

There wasn't quite the stigma attached to divorce in 1972 that there had been two decades before. However, this time Betty had children to think of, and that caused her a good deal of pain.

Betty moved out of the house she shared with Elliott and moved with Ellen to an apartment in the New Orleans suburb of Metairie, just west of the city—a neighborhood not unlike the one she'd just left. Vance didn't come with them: He was already eighteen and finished with high school, while Ellen was just beginning.

Although Elliott was the one who finally filed for divorce a year later, he didn't fight for custody and amicably left Ellen in Betty's care. He was given liberal visitation rights and contributed toward Ellen's support.

Ellen enrolled in Grace King High School, and from the very start she was quite happy there. Increasing maturity plus being out on her own forced Ellen to emerge as an individual; being more outgoing was also the only way she was able to make friends quickly.

Yet it was more than just the different scenery and new acquaintances that caused Ellen to change.

"My mother was going through some really hard times," Ellen remembers, "and I could see when she was really getting down, and I would start to make fun of her dancing. Then she'd start to laugh and I'd make fun of her laughing. And she'd laugh so hard she'd start to cry, and then I'd make fun of that. So I would totally bring her from where I'd seen her start going into depression to all the way out of it.

"As a thirteen-year-old kid, I learned I could manipulate people that way. That's a really powerful thing. But also, I saw I could make somebody happy. And my mother was someone whom I idolized. She's my mother, yet I'm changing her."

Ellen was quick to apply her newfound skills at

school, entertaining her schoolmates with impressions of teachers or other students, or coming up with outrageous excuses for kids who didn't do their homework. One student recalls Ellen suggesting that she sprinkle milk on old homework and leave it in the sun for a few hours. She reasoned that the stench would be such that the teacher wouldn't linger and so wouldn't notice that the assignment had been recycled.

Humor accelerated the process that had begun when Ellen moved, making her confident and accepted by her peers. To say that she enjoyed their attention is an understatement: Ellen told *Gambit* magazine, "I was hanging out with people who were older [and] staying out late."

And she was loving it—a little *too* much, as it turned out.

As before, Betty wasn't a single woman for very long.

Enjoying her freedom is one thing; being alone is quite another. No sooner was her divorce from Elliott finalized than Betty married Roy Gruessendorf, who bought rights-of-way for the electric company.

Ellen had grown remarkably independent during the year, developing into an attractive young woman, going out with friends of both sexes, playing a lot of tennis, and having a good old time. Being so close to New Orleans made it easy to do just about anything she wanted. And the appearance of a strong-willed stepfather who was big on responsibility and didn't particularly approve of her crowd gave her the reason to do so. More often than not, Ellen preferred to be anywhere but home.

At the same time, the teenager was increasingly concerned about where her life was headed. Other kids were *interested* in things: They wanted to be saxophonists, fashion designers, deejays, homemakers, attorneys, any number of things. Ellen had no idea what she wanted to do. Despite her outward self-assurance, she felt increasingly troubled.

"I had a lot of different friends," she says, "but all the time I was trying to find myself. I didn't know who I really wanted to be—or what I wanted to be."

Betty recognized and understood her daughter's confusion; to a degree, she was still experiencing it herself.

What do I want to do, and where do I want to do it?

Betty didn't see her having a new husband as the center of her life. She was terribly uncomfortable with Ellen's increasingly rebellious lifestyle, and after talking it over with Roy, she dropped a second bombshell.

Shortly after the marriage, while Ellen was still in her junior year at Grace King, Betty told her daughter that they were moving again. Not to New Orleans or somewhere else in the suburbs, not even to somewhere else in the state. This time the family was moving to Atlanta—Atlanta, *Texas,* not Georgia.

At first, like most teenagers, Ellen was profoundly upset by having to leave her friends and an area she knew and loved. For a time, she actually entertained the notion of moving in with her maternal grandmother, who lived in New Orleans.

A trip to Atlanta, however, along with encouragement from Betty, helped Ellen to focus on the positive: They'd have a nice home in Texas, her new school was small and modern and—most important—had a tennis team, the kids seemed genuinely personable, and Ellen would be able to visit her old stomping grounds during vacations.

And there was one thing more. The town was square—not a lot of long hair or outrageous fashions. Ellen resolved to change things once she got there—"the original *Footloose,*" one of her Atlanta neighbors describes her—by introducing everything from women's lib to the faddy, neon-bright Hot Sox.

The move *was* disruptive, but Ellen was determined to get through it without slipping into her old wallflower ways—and by counting the days until graduation.

4

Lone Star's State

*Texas . . . where the men rope cows and the
women run the place!*

—Molly Ivins

Atlanta, Texas, presently a town of 6,200 residents,
is situated some twenty-five miles south of Texarkana on U.S. Highway 59, a short trek northwest of
the point where Texas, Arkansas, and Louisiana
meet. Until Ellen became a celebrity, the best-
known citizens from around these parts were the
Texas Giants, the four Shields brothers who hailed
from nearby Greenville at the turn of the century.
While Ellen may be big, these boys were *really* big:
Each stood a quarter-inch under eight feet tall and
toured with the Ringling Bros. Circus.

Pine trees flourish in and around this quiet, very
green town of clear water and clean air. Nestled
comfortably in the Sun Belt, residents get the four
seasons—but only enough to have fun with them.

Winter temperatures rarely drop below fifty degrees, and the summers are hot but dry. Humid New Orleans it isn't.

Most of the residents who don't work for the timber industry or one of the community's eleven manufacturing plants are employed by the Texas Highway Department, whose district office is located in Atlanta.

When Ellen, Betty, and Roy arrived from Metairie, the population of Atlanta was just five thousand. Everyone may not have known everyone else here, but it was a town of one or two degrees of separation at most.

To put it mildly, the town was nothing like bustling New Orleans. Ellen says that it had "a downtown a block long. No building was taller than one story, and you hung out at the loop—which was the Dairy Queen." She adds that for teenage girls at that time, "the height of aspirations was to get your name in iridescent letters on the back of your boyfriend's pickup truck."

Though Ellen is being slightly facetious, the locals did tend to hold fairly modest goals, and the activities available to an Atlanta teen *were* on the thin side. There was only one movie theater, the sumptuous State, which has since closed down; before cable TV arrived just a few years ago, there were only three channels and, more often than not, reception was merely adequate. There was fishing, and Ellen did that with Roy from time to time, but she didn't enjoy it much.

For many kids, the most popular activity was

hanging around in City Park; the Dairy Queen parking lot was fine at night but too hot during the day. Kids just talked, listened to eight tracks, or listened to more eight tracks. Bands like Queen and the Tubes weren't big in Atlanta; Willie Nelson, Waylon Jennings, and the new Outlaw movement were.

It was also difficult for a teenager to get alcohol in Atlanta. Many adults didn't approve of liquor for adults, let alone for kids, and Ellen says they had to drive some forty-five miles whenever they wanted a beer.

"And," she told *Gambit,* "when you got there you didn't want to get just a six-pack since you'd driven all that far, so you got a case."

Case firmly in hand, Ellen and her new Texas buddies would then find a big empty field, build a bonfire, and drink until the small hours of the night.

She says that many kids got high by licking frogs. "Thank God this didn't catch on," she adds, "Can you picture going to a trendy bar, people standing around with a frog in their hand?"

But drinking (and frog-licking) was still done in secret, and kids didn't come back ready to shoot up the town. Young people at that time and in that place didn't cause mischief: Atlantans wouldn't have tolerated it.

A large segment of the young population held part-time jobs after school, as the work ethic was (and is) strong here. Other kids participated in the numerous activities organized by the local churches, from Bible studies to field trips to the popular youth choruses, which gave concerts as far away as New York and Hawaii.

Still others, like Ellen, took full advantage of the activities that were offered by the school.

Roy moved his family into a charming old home on Taylor Street, just off Main Street in the southwestern corner of the town. It's one of the oldest residential areas in Atlanta, and though somewhat rundown today, it was one of the loveliest at the time.

Atlanta High School is housed in a modern, single-story building that was just three years old when Ellen transferred there. Located in the northeastern section of Atlanta, the population of the school was six hundred, approximately three-quarters white and the rest black. Though nearly forty percent of the students rode the bus each morning, Ellen was usually driven to school by Roy on his way to work.

Although many transfer students have a tendency to hang back until they get the lay of the land, Ellen hit the ground running, just as she'd planned. Though she was somewhat overweight at the time —having been consoling herself with food—the five-foot-eight blond teenager didn't let that hold her back. Even when she became depressed about being away from the place she considered home, she forced herself to be outgoing and cheerful. Even when she didn't feel like it, she flashed those arresting blue eyes and a big smile that, even today, are what people tend to see first and remember.

And then there was her sense of humor.

"If you're pretty and you need something," Ellen says, "you play on your looks." Instead, she says, "I was funny and I used that to fit in."

Did she ever. "What a gift from God that was," says Jimmy, a close friend of Betty. "Her mother loved it and so did Ellen's friends. Humor was always in the air around her, like a refreshing breeze."

Assistant Principal Sidney Harrist, who was a teacher at the time, says the word "gregarious" springs to mind whenever he thinks about Ellen— though "not in a negative sense. Ellen was impulsive in a very warm and charming way. She had no trouble making friends quickly, and she had no trouble keeping them. Nor can I recall her ever saying a cross word about anyone."

He says that she always had a smile, a twinkle in her eye, and a "propensity for finding the comical in everything." She never did anything outlandish or rude—at least not in school. Friends and teachers remember Ellen doing things like playing with a sandwich at lunch while doing voices as though it were a Muppet or pretending to be a pine tree begging for mercy.

English teacher Ruth Trumble, who taught Ellen in her senior year, agrees with Harrist about the young woman's endearing qualities. She says that she really "enjoyed having her in my class" because Ellen was not only a very good student, but she had a splendid sense of humor. Not that she was the class-clown type: As Trumble told reporter Mark Thompson of the local *Citizens Journal,* "She was really rather quiet in class, but she had a shy, sly grin." The teacher likens the smile to that of the Cheshire Cat from *Alice in Wonderland.* Even though Ellen didn't say much, Trumble could tell that her mind was always working. Trumble adds, "I'm really pleased with what she's done."

Student Kim Miller, who was in her sophomore year when Ellen was a senior, told the *Citizens Journal* that Ellen "always had an upbeat attitude and a smile on her face. She also had a great sense of humor, even back then. She was always the center of attention. When I see her on television, it's just the same character she was in high school. The very same character." Echoing the words of Ellen's friend from La Salle Elementary School, Miller also observes, with a trace of jealousy, "She hasn't aged a bit. I don't know what her secret is."

Ellen was also very active in after-school activities, participating in as many as she could. She was especially fond of singing in the chorus, and she was a varsity tennis star for two years with the school team, the Rabbits. She won the team's Outstanding Player Award as a junior, though she lost as a senior to friend and rival Gladys Johnson.

But Ellen doesn't hold a grudge. Now a teacher and a coach in the Dallas suburb of Richardson,

Johnson remains a very close friend of hers, and the two get together whenever they can.

Johnson reveals that although Ellen never once gave a thought to the notion of being a comedian, she was very adept at it.

"If anybody was ever meant to be a comedian, she was," Johnson says. Not only did Ellen have a quick wit, she had the ability to establish an instant rapport with anyone who was around her, under any circumstances.

But by far the greatest rapport Ellen formed with anyone in high school was with tall, handsome Ben Heath. The two of them became close friends late in their junior year, and the blond, hunky football star literally swept Ellen off her feet. Apart from their shared interest in athletics, the studious, sincere, very caring Heath really enjoyed Ellen's sense of humor. Acquaintances describe Ben as also having been just a little gullible, and Ellen used to lead him on with "What?! You didn't study for the big test?" type put-ons.

Then as now, Ellen was a huge movie buff. On one of their first dates in 1975, they went to see *Return of the Pink Panther,* and Heath recalls that "she laughed all the way through it." The star of the film, Peter Sellers, became a big hero of Ellen's, and one can clearly see his droll Inspector Clouseau character in her own understated delivery.

Heath also remembers that when they were able to get the brand-new *Saturday Night Live* on TV, they both became big fans of the show, and Chevy Chase in particular. (Among leading men, Heath says that Ellen was extremely partial to Warren Beatty.)

Ellen was infatuated with Heath, he adored her, and as the end of their senior year approached she very much wanted to marry him. The feeling was mutual. Heath says that the two of them "were serious about each other."

Heath was going to go away to college, however, and after a great deal of soul-searching, Ellen recalls, "He told me he thought we should wait." Which meant, she knew at the time, that it wasn't going to be.

Ellen had no choice but to agree, and the high-school romance ended. The woman who eventually became Heath's wife, Debbie, says, "It broke Ellen's heart."

Still married and employed by Douglassville Timber, Heath admits that he often thinks of Ellen, remembering her as "really just a nice, outgoing person. She was real entertaining and lots of fun to talk to." Ellen's success comes as no surprise to Heath either: "I've known it was coming for a long time now."

Instead of becoming Mrs. Heath, as she'd hoped, Ellen had nothing to look forward to when she graduated. She had no desire to go to college, no job, and no goals. Apart from her sense of humor, in fact, all she had going for her was her mother.

Betty Gruessendorf was something of an oddity in Atlanta.

Employed as a secretary at Guardline Industries,

a manufacturer of safety apparel, Betty drove to work every day on a motor scooter, drove all the way to Texarkana to take her beloved violin lessons, and each and every day used her lunch hour to walk four brisk miles—years before jogging and fitness were a national craze. This was indicative of the woman's independent streak, which many local women found off-putting. Though they found her charming and genuinely kind, and many of them liked her, many refused to associate with her lest they too be considered odd. They were also intimidated by her intelligence and remarkable poise. They felt that *she* felt she was better than they were.

That wasn't Betty's style at all. Her friend Jimmy, who worked alongside her at Guardline, says, "She was the most caring person I ever met. She and Ellen used to have an open house at Christmas, set out food and treats for anyone who cared to come by." Jimmy feels that people may have been "jealous" of how confident and self-motivated Betty was.

For her part, Betty may have envied many of the women who spurned her: More than anything, she wished she had a family as tight and loving as those of many of the other women she knew.

But that was a private dream, no longer possible and best filed under the "wouldn't it have been nice" category. A more immediate problem, one that never left her, was concern over her daughter's future.

Despite her grave disappointment over losing Ben Heath, Ellen's life has never been governed by the approval of anyone but her mother. That was particularly true in her relationship with Roy, a courteous, even courtly man who never really understood the burning need his wife and step-daughter had to be so independent.

There wasn't much that Roy could do to change his wife's ways, especially after she'd lived in the relatively tolerant environment of New Orleans. But he tried very hard to help his stepdaughter as best he could by suggesting schools or jobs or even beaus for her.

Ellen resisted his input. People who knew the family say that she never really accepted Roy as a father figure and probably wouldn't have taken his advice regardless of what it was. She didn't want to go to college, and the idea of being a secretary or assembly-line worker held no appeal for her—not because she felt she was too good for that, she was simply too restless and inquisitive. Her disappoint-ment with Ben appears to have strengthened her determination to be as self-reliant as her mother or grandmother.

Roy and Betty argued regularly about Ellen, who was unhappy about adding stress to her mother's life.

"I think my parents were very worried about me," Ellen says, and admits that they had good reasons to be. Traditional jobs just weren't for her.

"I worked in a glove factory for about a day and a half. My mother worked there, and I remember midday the second day I said, 'I'm not feeling well. I'm going to go home.' She said, 'You're not coming back, are you?' I said, 'No.' And so I never came back. I worked jobs like that, for a day or two."

But while Ellen didn't want a traditional future, she didn't know *what* she wanted. And while a lot of teenagers feel that way, Ellen, as one friend put it, "seemed to be running from the idea of conformity. She wanted to do something that people either didn't expect from her *or* from a woman, or else after hearing about it would say, 'Hey, that's neat!' "

She would have loved to play tennis but knew that she wasn't good enough. She also enjoyed golf but didn't see how she could make a living at it. She had a great time whenever she was singing, but she didn't see herself as a threat to Bette Midler.

The only thing she did know was that she'd never find a life for herself in Atlanta and intended to get out of town the day after she graduated.

5

Homeward Bound

If you obey all the rules you miss all the fun.

—Katharine Hepburn

Ellen's frustration intensified during the spring of 1976 as she adjusted to the idea of life without Ben, as Roy kept after her to get a job, and as she became more and more depressed about her uncertain future. She felt as if she were being pounded emotionally and spiritually, and hitting around a tennis ball or getting drunk wasn't the kind of outlet she needed.

Ellen later said of her life, "Sometimes you feel, 'Is it just me who wants to have fun and not take life so seriously?'"

Throughout these long and trying months, Betty ached for her daughter.

Ellen tried to stay out at night as much as possible so that she wouldn't argue with Roy; when they *were* together, Betty tried (and failed) to smooth things over between them, but even she got tired and exasperated playing referee. These "discussions" sometimes ended with Ellen storming out, Betty running after her daughter, and the two of them going for long walks and talking things out. Ellen hated how these blowups caught her mother in the middle, but she also hated being talked to like she was still a kid.

Betty agreed that Ellen wouldn't find contentment in Atlanta but didn't know where she could go. Without a college education, without any real skills, her daughter would find it rough anywhere she went.

The problem was never far from Betty's mind. At work she would often fall silent and stare out the window for hours each day. She felt that Ellen had enormous potential to make something of herself. Jimmy Wade says that more than once, the words "star" and "Ellen" were connected. Betty believed that Ellen could be a professional athlete if she tried, or that she could be a politician or an entertainer because she was so good with people. Betty had always hoped that Ellen might even take up an instrument, get serious about the singing she did in chorus, or even consider acting. Ellen had what Betty felt were the keys to succeeding in any of these areas: "a very positive attitude and a joyous spirit."

But Ellen was unmotivated and unfocused, and Betty knew that she needed someone to help her, to guide her. As Betty often said to Jimmy, "I think that I could help her develop her skills, but I can't be with her if she leaves. . . . And she is going to leave, I'm sure."

After some long-distance phone calls, Ellen finally decided where she'd be going: back to New Orleans to live with her grandmother. Betty was sad that they wouldn't be together, though she was relieved that at least Ellen would be with family.

The night before Ellen left was graduation night. She came home from a party and finished loading her yellow Volkswagen with all her worldly possessions: clothes, records, stereo, boxes of books, and a few mementos. The next morning, before Ellen began on the three-hundred-mile drive to New Orleans, her mother ate breakfast with her and then walked her to the car.

"Try whatever you want to try until you find what makes you happy," Betty told her, tears in her eyes, "and don't ever be afraid of failing."

Ellen hugged her mother and said she'd be fine. She also said she hoped her mother would find ways to make herself happier.

Betty didn't bother to tell her daughter that she would always be welcome back in Atlanta: Ellen knew that. Betty did tell her to write or call if she needed anything, however, even though she knew that Ellen—proud and increasingly defiant— would sooner do without than ask for help.

Soon after Ellen left, Roy and Betty moved to a new house just off Williams Street, on the corner of Live Oak and White Oak streets, right beside a nursing home. It was a smaller home, and Betty may have felt it would be easier to adjust to this next phase of her life if she weren't constantly reminded of Ellen.

But there was no escaping the fact that she sorely missed her daughter. When Ellen left, Jimmy recalls that Betty was rather moody: She was up when Ellen wrote or called, then down again. Jimmy was virtually all that Betty had in the way of a friend, and the two spent a lot of time together, going to the movies, doing volunteer typing at the church she attended regularly, or even driving over the state border to listen to Vance play guitar with his band at clubs in Shreveport (home of the legendary Paula Records, where keyboardist Thomas DeGeneres did all of his recording with John Fred and His Playboy Band.)

It was especially important to Betty that she be there for Vance at this time, because he was involved in a lawsuit involving profit participation in an enormously popular character he had co-created—a lawsuit that had drained him financially and emotionally.

One night in 1977, he and his friends Walter Williams and David Derickson were horsing around and they came up with an idea for a short movie, which they shot and submitted to *Saturday Night Live*. The show's producers loved the film and decided to air it. The modest little effort was called "Home Movie" and subtitled "The Mr. Bill Show."

"Hoo-hoo, kiddies," the red, white, and blue clay figure cheers in his first appearance. "It's so good to

see all your bright faces out in front of the TV set."
After introducing his helper, Mr. Hands—played
by Vance—Mr. Bill watches in horror as his soiled
dog Spot is cleaned by being dropped in boiling
water. Then the sadistic Mr. Sluggo comes to visit,
running over Mr. Bill with his convertible.

Audiences loved the short, and the producers
commissioned more films starring the small brutal-
ized figure.

(When the lawsuit was behind him and Vance
was able to concentrate on his music, he scored two
back-to-back songwriting hits with "Middle of Nowhere" for the film *Bull Durham* and "Walk in My
Sleep" for *The Accused,* both in 1988.)

Ellen was thrilled for her brother and very sup-
portive of him during his subsequent legal troubles.
She was also a little envious: not of what he'd done,
but the fact that he'd been motivated to do anything at all.

She hoped that New Orleans would help her find
a Mr. Bill of her own.

6

Funny Girl

I'm going to write a book about the South. I'm going to call it When Beautiful Places Happen to Bad People.

—Brett Butler

After she'd settled in with her grandmother, Ellen searched through the want ads, looked up old friends to see what they were doing, and still didn't have a clue as to what she wanted to do. During the day she looked for work; at night, she hung out with friends at bars—including gay bars for a change of pace. She found the company of women stimulating, deep, and honest, and she began to spend more and more time with them.

She took a succession of jobs—what she called "an odd-job binge"—holding each one for hours, weeks, or months, depending on how quickly she became bored, restless, or self-conscious.

She worked as an employment counselor, wrapped packages in a department store (which later inspired the wrapper's rap she used in her early act), took a job as a clothing salesperson, and tried tending bar and waitressing. She shucked oysters, painted houses, and sold vacuum cleaners. She even went to work as a landscaper, though the job lasted four hours (she'd thought she'd be watering lawns, not mowing them). Totally *not* mechanically inclined, Ellen was afraid she'd cut off a toe. Worse, she would be doing it "on a busy street where my friends might see me."

She had only slightly more success as a vacuum cleaner salesperson for Hoover. She recalls, "I'd go to different stores and demonstrate when people were shopping. I'd throw mud in front of them. That's what I did. Boy, did that job suck. That was one of my first jokes when I started doing comedy. I would use humor to sell. I was so good with just coming up with something. The most expensive vacuum cleaner had a light on the front of it. And I was trying to make that sale. And the woman said, 'Why do I need a light on the front of a vacuum cleaner?' And I said, 'That's so you can vacuum at night and not wake up people by turning the lights on.' She bought it."

Ellen liked the outdoor work better than the indoor work, liked physical labor better than selling. But none of it had that this-is-what-I-want-to-do-with-the-rest-of-my-life feel.

As much as Ellen's grandmother gave her the love and support she needed, Ellen realized that she wasn't getting the motivation she needed. There was only one person who could give her that. Whether it was the self-imposed pressure of trying to be the best at tennis, or getting through the breakup with Heath, Ellen was always encouraged and strengthened by long talks with her mother.

Though Betty came to visit now and then, and Ellen went home on the holidays, it wasn't the same. More than that, it wasn't enough. After three years of living in New Orleans, the twenty-one-year-old was in the same rut she'd been in after graduating from high school. She needed to get away, to get some perspective on her life. Once again cramming everything into her aging Beetle, she hit the road and headed for home.

When Ellen pulled up in front of Guardline Industries, Betty had no idea that she was coming. Her daughter just slid from the packed car (a Guardline employee recalls, "You couldn't have fit a piece of straw in there") and shambled in, hot and tired from the long ride. She walked over to Betty, who literally gasped when she saw Ellen, and then the two of them cried their eyes out.

Finally tearing herself away, Betty finished up a few things at the office and went home with her daughter.

The two talked through the night, Ellen telling her that all she'd discovered in New Orleans were the things she *didn't* want to do. She needed time to think, and Betty said she'd be only too happy to give it to her.

That night, Ellen also asked her mother if *she* were happy.

Betty thought for a minute. She told Ellen that

she wasn't unhappy—though if she had it all to do over again, her first priority might have been to find a career that was rewarding. She said that if you aren't fulfilled and challenged by what you're doing day after day, you'll never be truly content.

However, they both knew that the kind of challenge Ellen needed was not to be found in Atlanta. She didn't want to be cooped up in an office or restaurant, so she applied for a job with the state highway department: There was a lot of construction going on at the time, and she hoped she could get a job holding up stop signs at construction sites.

She was turned down.

Depressed and a little annoyed, she looked up old friends, hung out around town, and managed to aggravate Roy with her seeming lack of ambition. He felt she should get a job, any job; an honest day's work, a restful night at home, and a weekend of golf or some other recreation was his idea of life as it should be lived. In that respect, he was not much different from the rest of the citizens of Atlanta. The town already thought Betty was something of a wild woman, and that Vance was an eccentric. Ellen only added to the oddball reputation.

Betty's willingness to put up with Ellen's lifestyle also bothered Roy. He didn't understand why she wouldn't lean on her daughter, and there were more than a few heated discussions about how long the young woman was going to be allowed to stay at home and do nothing.

The answer was seven months.

Ellen didn't work much the entire time she was

in Atlanta, though she wasn't idle. Toward the end, she began to write. She wanted to try and sell humorous pieces to some of the hot new magazines like *Ms.* or *The National Lampoon.* However, when Ellen saw that her presence back at home was forcing her mother to side with her against Roy, she decided it was time to leave.

Ellen packed the car once more, only this time leaving room for her mother. Taking a three-month leave from her job, Betty went to New Orleans with Ellen. They stayed with Ellen's grandmother until they found her a furnished apartment, which Ellen rented with a slightly older woman, and while Ellen went job-hunting Betty came over and cleaned the place until it was spotless, even dusting behind the pictures hanging on the wall.

Betty also helped Ellen adjust to yet another change in her life. Though Ellen has never said anything for the record about her relationship with her roommate, friends say that it quickly went from "like" to "trust" to "love." Encouraged by the liberal environment of New Orleans, the women were open in their affection, and Ellen found herself very much at ease in a new lifestyle.

Ellen continued writing in her free time, though there was nothing that she liked enough to send out. The stuff sat in a drawer or was sent back to Atlanta, where her mother read it and proudly showed it off to her few friends.

On the job—whichever job it happened to be— Ellen kept her spirits up by slipping easily into her old, joking high-school ways. She liked the process of listening, quickly turning something over in her mind, and coming up with a quip or observation that made someone laugh—as long as it was mild enough not to get her fired.

After a few weeks of this, more than one of Ellen's co-workers told her that she ought to try her hand at stand-up. And as it happened, the opportunity presented itself to do just that.

She doesn't remember exactly who, what, or why, but says, "The first time I got onstage was for some benefit, around 1980. Somebody needed to raise money for something and no one had access to Eddie Murphy or Aerosmith, so they put a band together and asked me to get onstage someplace in the French Quarter and be funny.

"I don't even remember if there *was* a stage," she says. "In fact, I don't think that anyone had ever worked a mike before—or a sound system. It was one of those let's-put-on-a-show-in-a-barn things."

"Terrified at first" and convinced that she'd get booed off the stage, Ellen only bothered to prepare one bit. On her way to the venue, she bought a Burger King Whopper, french fries, and a shake, went onstage, and started telling a story—about what, she doesn't remember.

She told *Gambit,* "I always thought it was funny when people have something to tell you and they take a huge bite of something, and then they make you wait to finish that bite. And then when they're halfway through the sentence, they take another huge bite.

"So I got onstage and said, 'I gotta tell you about the funniest thing that happened to me the other day. But I'm sorry, this is the only chance I'm going to get to sit down and eat today, so if you don't mind I'm going to eat my lunch.'"

She started to tell her story, then took a bite of Whopper and chewed.

"I'd finish that," she remembers, "then start a new sentence, take another huge bite—that was back in the days I didn't mind eating tortured animals—and by the time I finished everything I looked at my watch and said, 'Oh, my time is up. Gotta go.' Then I left. I'd gotten maybe ten words out."

She says that while the material wouldn't be funny today, the experience was incredible: "I loved it. It was just the greatest feeling."

The thunderous applause took her completely by surprise, as did some people in the audience who came up to her after the show. They were impressed with her performance and with her stage presence, and they asked her if she'd like to come and work at a coffeehouse located near the University of New Orleans.

Caught off-guard again, Ellen said sure, she'd love to do that. They selected a date for her to start—just a few days hence—and only as she drove home did Ellen wonder about the wisdom of what she'd committed herself to do.

When she got to the apartment, and she and her roommate looked over the things she'd been putting on paper, her confidence soared. Ellen realized that a lot of her stories and observations just might work better if they were delivered from behind a microphone.

Okay, she thought.

She had the material. She had the venue. She had the motivation. The real question was, did she have the gumption to actually get out there and do it?

There was only one way to find out.

7

Ellen and Clyde

Adults are always asking little kids what they want to be when they grow up because they're looking for ideas.

—Paula Poundstone

Ellen remembers emotional chaos extremely well. She also remembers very well her early days and weeks as a fledgling stand-up.

Ellen says that the first time she went onstage at the coffeehouse she was "afraid," which is not surprising: She says she "didn't have many minutes" of material. But she dealt with her fear the way stand-ups have always dealt with stage fright: by going on anyway. And not only did Ellen overcome her fear, she was an immediate success.

She continued doing her food bit, which worked very well with the *Animal House* crowd that came to the coffeehouse, and also talked about the value of higher education: Without it, she told the kids, you'll end up eating Whoppers on coffeehouse stages. She also talked about drinking, about relationships, and reminisced about her childhood.

"I was coming home from kindergarten—well," she said, "they told me it was kindergarten. I found out later I had been working in a factory for ten years. It's good for a kid to know how to make gloves."

Her set was short and tight, and it brought the house down each time she appeared. What she realized in those early days, she says, is "that people laughed at me because of the way I was, naturally. I figured if I could, onstage, be the same kind of person I am offstage, then it would work."

It worked, all right. She was so successful that she also landed gigs at nearby Tulane University.

Though Ellen was still working at various jobs during the day and was doing comedy "as a joke," her Atlanta friend Gladys Johnson says that "people laughed at her, and she was encouraged to come back, again and again."

Gladys came to New Orleans to catch one of Ellen's earliest performances and remembers being thoroughly impressed by the material, by Ellen's confidence, and by the audience reaction. Though it was just a week or two after Ellen had first gotten behind the microphone at the club, Gladys says that by this time not only was her old friend not nervous any more, she really seemed to be having a great time, thriving on the audience feedback.

Ellen *was* having fun, and she had finally found a place where she felt she really belonged, where she felt comfortable and challenged.

And then, Ellen recalls, her life changed when, "out of nowhere, the comedy club opened up."

For a long time, Clyde's Comedy Corner in the French Quarter wasn't just *the* humor showcase in New Orleans, it was literally the *only* comedy showcase for local talents to try out their routines.

When Clyde's Comedy Corner opened, "out of nowhere," says Ellen, she was one of the first stand-ups hired by owner Clyde Abercrombie.

"[Clyde's] was like a lot of places in the Quarter," says an attorney who prepared the incorporation papers for the club, which was located at 300 Bourbon Street. He says that it was "small, smoky, and dark.

"But it was quite popular for a while and made a local name for itself as a place to go if you wanted to hear known stand-ups or were brave enough to get up and perform as an unknown [on amateur night]."

Ellen agreed to do one show a night during the week and two a night on Fridays and Saturdays.

"I was so excited to be working at all," Ellen says, "I don't think I noticed that some nights there were only [a few] people sitting out there. To me, it was a packed house."

Even better, as she told *Gambit* magazine, "I was making three hundred dollars a week." Which meant that Ellen was earning enough that she could quit her day job—though she doesn't happen to remember what it was at the time.

The college audiences had pretty much been the same from night to night, and during the first few weeks of working at Clyde's, Ellen learned the basics of playing to different types of audiences each night, people of different ages and from different economic groups. She learned by trial and error and, of course, by watching others.

She mastered the art of keeping her delivery slow, which suggests confidence and also allows the performer to gauge audience reaction and adjust. She learned how to draw the audience in by talking to individual members, loosening them up, making them part of the act.

The most important thing she learned in these initial forays was to be true to herself. For Ellen, the rule of thumb was to "keep it clean, get rid of the filth, and just be yourself." Buddy Morra, one of the top managers of stand-ups in the business, says that every successful comic learns what Ellen learned early on: "You shouldn't give an audience what *they* want. Give them what *you* want."

At first, Ellen transferred her act virtually intact from the college sites, and within a matter of days she discovered what worked and what didn't with the diverse group that patronized Clyde's. She wrote new material, some of it based on the behavior of the more unusual patrons of the club, some of it coming from her childhood.

She says, for instance, that she remembers being four or five and her father asking her, "Ellen, what would you like for Christmas?"

She said, "Gosh, Dad, what I'd really like is a dolly."

On Christmas Day, she says, "He wheels in this

tremendous metal thing. Y'ever try to dress one of those things? They're impossible."

She went on to say that they had fire drills in her house, and everyone was assigned objects they were supposed to save: Her father grabbed the pets, her mother the jewelry, her brother was supposed to run and get help, and Ellen was supposed "to try to save the washer and dryer." She adds, "Good thing I had that dolly."

The rest of her new material consisted primarily of observations about spending one's teenage years in a small town, the differences between Atlanta and New Orleans, and what it was like living with her grandmother. ("My grandmother started walking five miles a day when she was sixty. She's ninety-three today and we don't know where the hell she is." This quickly became something of a signature line for Ellen, and she's still using it in her act.)

Alas, one of the first bits to go was the successful talking-with-a-mouthful-of-Whopper. Even though Ellen loved it and it always got laughs, she says she was forced to drop it. "I knew instinctively I couldn't just keep eating onstage. 'Oh, hey, it's that girl who eats onstage. Gee, she's huge!'"

When Ellen started her tenure at Clyde's, she began as the evening's opener, doing ten, then fifteen, then twenty minutes. After proving herself, she moved up to the middle spot with thirty minutes, and finally she was promoted to closing act. By the time Ellen ended her stay at the club, toward the end of 1981, she was not only staying onstage anywhere from forty-five to sixty minutes a night, she was also emceeing the other acts.

Unfortunately, Clyde and Ellen didn't always get along. He was a freewheeling, plain-speaking promoter who struck her as caring more about profit than about comedy. Though that wasn't entirely true, he was not above doing what it took to generate traffic.

Ellen's assessment of Clyde was reinforced when he decided that he could make money by adding a third show on Saturday night. He announced to his regular performers that he intended to make it a very late show—and one that was X-rated. He said that he wanted to appeal to the same crowd that went to any of the numerous Bourbon Street clubs with their nude dancing girls and erotic shows.

Ellen was deeply disturbed by this, even more when he said that he wanted her to be his X-rated "girl." Not to dance naked or anything, but to tell sex jokes and spice up her act with four-letter words and racy stories.

"I explained to him that I wasn't dirty," Ellen says. "He explained to me that I had to be dirty if I wanted to work there. And I explained to him that I would quit before I would be dirty."

Not wanting to lose someone who was a top drawer for his other shows, Clyde capitulated. He kept Ellen on and got another woman to do his dirty show.

It was a small victory, but after a couple of setbacks she was happy to have won something.

Unfortunately, she was about to suffer a loss that would overshadow anything she had experienced before—or since.

Ellen's immediate success at Clyde's was not good news in every way. Many of the other comics, most of whom had spent months and in some cases years behind a microphone, were jealous of her ability to form an instant bond with audiences and win them over.

She says, "All the people working in the club would get onstage and try to blow me away because they were angry and bitter that I didn't have the experience, and here I was surpassing them."

But she didn't let that faze her. For one thing, Ellen says that headliners who stopped by Clyde's to perform or just check out the competition "kept telling me I was good enough to move to New York or Los Angeles or wherever." That did a lot to boost her confidence.

For another thing, for the first time in her life she had a sense of real accomplishment as well as a direction, a goal. She began to feel that with a year or two of experience under her belt, and a couple of world-class bits, she would never have to hold a day job again and could take a shot at making it in this business.

As it happens, getting where she was had been easy. The tough part was yet to come.

8

Ellen Wheels

If I had to live my life again, I'd make all the same mistakes—only sooner.

—Tallulah Bankhead

Ellen understood that at some point, usually very early in their career, comedians *have* to go on the road in order to become known. The rule of thumb these days is that it takes from four to seven years of relentless plugging before a stand-up can make a good living—in the $100,000 range—doing the comedy clubs, cruise ships, awards and industrial show circuit.

It wasn't always that way.

In the late teens and early 1920s, comedians made their "name and fame and boodle" on the legitimate vaudeville stage (or in bawdy burlesque, if they weren't quite as lucky). The most enduring of these entertainers, like Jack Benny, Abbott and Costello, and Bob Hope, went to radio in the 1930s and 1940s and then moved on to the movies. In the early 1950s it was television, though many of the stars were transplants from other media.

Things began to change in the middle and late 1950s, when stand-up comics and social satirists like Mort Sahl, Dick Gregory, George Kirby, Bob Newhart, Totie Fields, and Moms Mabley began to flourish. The process by which comedians made it in those days became fairly standardized rather quickly. The comics would leave their hometown and head to New York or Los Angeles and would try to make a name for themselves at the local night clubs or coffeehouses—which, more and more, the poets and beatniks were turning over to the stand-ups. They'd get themselves a solid reputation, a strong following, build up to a week or two in a top local club like the Cafe Wha? in Greenwich Village or the Purple Onion in L.A., and land a record contract when label executives came to hear them. The record contracts were especially important: Not only did it give them national exposure, but the labels were able to book them on variety shows like *The Ed Sullivan Show* or *The Tonight Show,* which perpetuated sales. Without them, comedians like Newhart, Bill Cosby, the Smothers Brothers, and Allan Sherman wouldn't have been able to sustain their place in the spotlight.

Not every comedian worked well on vinyl, of course, which is why the likes of Lord Buckley never got beyond their New York following, Jonathan Winters had to wait for TV to find him, and solid comics like Martin and Rossi were limited (lucrative though it was) to headlining in Las Vegas.

Not only was the evolution of the stand-up terribly formularized, but the material comedians came up with tended to be relatively mainstream. Sahl and Gregory had begun to test the boundaries with their political humor, Woody Allen flirted with sex, and the brilliant Lenny Bruce blazed trails (and got burned) for his uninhibited language and brilliant monologues.

(Typical was his classic bit about the Lone Ranger. As two townspeople watch the Masked Man ride off, one of them complains, "What's with that putz? The schmuck didn't wait! Mama made coffee and cake and everything—what the hell is *with* that guy? I've got my hand out like some jackoff, he's on his horse already. The Lone Ranger. So what the hell does *that* give him? What an asshole! I'm gonna punch the shit out of him if I ever see him again!" "Take it easy, Dominique—" "Take it easy my *balls*. Is that guy kiddin' me?" "You don't know about him? He's got a problem, goin' to analysis. He can't accept love. . . .")

Bruce was an exception. Anyone who wanted to go nationwide had to be clean. Bill Grundfest, who owned the Comedy Cellar in the Village, notes, "In those days . . . compromise was a necessity of the times." And Dick Gregory says that comics went along with it for the simple reason that "in 1961 you were putting cardboard in your shoes to keep out the cold, and in 1962 you have more shoes than you'll ever need."

Richard Pryor changed all of that when he

walked off a Las Vegas stage in 1970. He had been doing whitewashed material and finally said—onstage—"What the fuck am I doing here?" He left, spent several months writing honest and heartfelt routines, and came back—blunt, brutal, and funnier than any living human. He clicked in the clubs, on records, on TV, and in the movies: His 1979 stand-up film, *Richard Pryor—Live in Concert*, is one of the greatest sustained stand-up performances ever. Tim Allen recalls that this film "made me laugh so hard that I almost felt ill," and that after he saw it, "that's all I ever wanted to do, make somebody laugh that hard."

Pryor didn't only open the door for blue material to go mainstream, he made it possible for comics of every minority and gender to break through—and, equally important, to break through to the young.

By the late 1960s, there were other outlets for talented new comics as well. The Second City comedy and improvisational troupes in Chicago and Toronto helped to launch the careers of many comic actors, such as John and Jim Belushi, John Candy, Martin Short, and others. On TV, beginning in 1975, TV's *Saturday Night Live*—which included Second City alumni—became a breeding ground for comic actors.

But pure stand-ups were in something akin to limbo. By showing that there was another way, Pryor had pretty much destroyed the factorylike process that had spawned his generation of comics. It wasn't until the late 1970s, with the rise of cable

TV, that things began to change. Cable TV was free to use the kind of language broadcast TV couldn't and to deal with any kind of subject matter; and concert films like Pryor's, as well as performances by blunt, incisive stand-ups like George Carlin or off-the-wall comics like Steve Martin and Robin Williams, were pulling in big ratings for services like HBO and Showtime.

Cable hungered for timely, stand-up comedy, clubs like the Improv in L.A. were happy to provide it, and a new synergy was born. So was a new night out for young people: Their appetites whetted by TV, instead of going to the movies they would go to local comedy clubs. Soon the clubs, and their ubiquitous brick walls, were a fixture of towns from Anchorage, Alaska (Pierce Street Annex), to Wauwatosa, Wisconsin (Sir Laughs A Lot Comedy Castle).

And, of course, to New Orleans.

By the middle 1980s, there were nearly four hundred of these clubs nationwide.

It was into this environment of plenty that Ellen was considering throwing herself when she received a phone call from a friend. The woman had recently moved from New Orleans and told Ellen that she'd found the perfect place to live: San Francisco.

The friend said, "You won't believe this place. It's beautiful, there are comedy clubs everywhere, and you'd do very well here."

Always an adventurer, Ellen says that that call was all it took to convince her. Selling her car and shipping her few belongings west, she arranged to stay with her friend and two other girls, to give California a try.

Even though she hates flying ("Probably because I'm not in control"), Ellen flew out and says of her first impression of San Francisco that it was everything she'd hoped it would be.

"It was beautiful," she told *Gambit*. "When I got off the plane I had no idea the air could be like that. I thought everyone lived the way we did in New Orleans—sweating while they blow-dried their hair."

As she hugged her friend in the terminal, she felt she'd made the right decision in getting out of New Orleans and coming here.

However, the West Coast did not turn out to be everything Ellen had hoped for. Though she loved the city, and she was able to get spots at the comedy clubs, Ellen was now a very little fish in a very big pond. She didn't make much money doing stand-up, and that depressed her enormously.

"I was having to work a regular job," she remembers, and that seemed like a step in the wrong direction. Worse, she says, "after a couple of months I got homesick. I wanted to come back to New Orleans."

So she did, moving in again with her old roommate.

But things weren't quite the same in New Orleans. Ellen didn't want to go back to work at Clyde's: The club was having financial problems and, indeed, would end up closing shortly thereafter. (Years later, Ellen seemed remarkably ambivalent and even a little bitter about her old stomping grounds. She says she honestly and truly has "no idea" where it was located, though she believes she'll "find out eventually—it will all come back in therapy.")

Besides, by that time the foul-mouthed acts had pretty much taken over. It wasn't an environment that could do her any good.

She would have to get a day job yet again, and, not surprisingly, something approaching the old fears returned to haunt her.

If she were serious about being a comedian, she *had* to go on the road. She'd always known that. But what if the rest of the country were like San Francisco: lots of stand-ups and low pay for newcomers, and even lower pay for female newcomers? How would she earn a living? Go from job to job like Richard Kimble? Who would hire her for just a week or two?

She needed to figure it all out—though, as it often does, fate and tragedy helped her find her way.

9

A Phone Call
to God

*It takes a long while for a naturally trustful
person to reconcile himself to the idea that,
after all, God will not help him.*

—H. L. Mencken

Since she had to make money quickly, Ellen took
the only job she could get: working as a gofer at a
Storyville law firm, making coffee, making photo-
copies, and making very little salary.

"When I was working at the law firm," she says,
"I really tried to tell those people that I was a
comedian and they'd say, 'Sure you are. . . . Now
go make the coffee.'

"And I would have to make the coffee and do the
Xeroxing and fit into that little world that I have
never felt I was a part of."

Depressed and disappointed, Ellen would ride
the bus to and from work and use that time to write
new material.

One day, the bus slowed and Ellen glanced out the window as they passed a fatal car wreck. The bus inched by, past glass and twisted bits of metal everywhere. The terrible accident brought Ellen down even further, though it wasn't until she got home and received a phone call from the police that she learned who the victim had been: her roommate, who had been out on a date.

Ellen was devastated beyond words. A close friend of hers at the time says, "Ellen was just grief-stricken. She couldn't believe someone could be ripped out of your life without any warning, was gone, never to be seen or talked to again. It really destroyed her.

"Ellen had really been in love with this woman. Even though the sexual relationship ultimately ended, they remained good friends—but Ellen apparently still carried a torch for the woman.

"So it was a double trauma to lose both a friend and someone she was in love with. It took Ellen a long time to get over her death, and after she did it's almost as if Ellen dedicated her success to the woman."

The friend adds, "To this day, she's very protective of the woman's memory—she wouldn't want any negative things said about her or people to think badly of her."

For that reason, she does not want her name published: She doesn't want the tabloid press digging up her body and putting a tawdry spin on what was a very private and very emotional relationship.

* * *

Despite the enormity of her loss, Ellen had to deal with practical matters, such as where she was going to live. Not only was she unable to afford the apartment by herself, but she also wasn't sure she wanted to stay in a place so ripe with memories.

She moved into a small room in a poor section of town—"a flea-ridden apartment in a basement," as she describes it, with only a mattress to sleep on and a few sticks of furniture. Ellen says she remembers just lying there, night after night, unable to sleep and staring at the ceiling.

As she later revealed in a moving interview with *The New York Times,* "I'm lying on the floor, wide awake, thinking, 'Here's this beautiful girl, twenty-three years old, who's just gone. So I started writing what it would be like to call God and ask why fleas are here and this person is not. But my mind just kicked into what all of a sudden would happen if you actually picked up the phone and called God. How it would take forever, how it would ring for a long time because . . . it's a big place. And it was like something came through me. I remember writing it nonstop, not thinking what would happen next. And when I finished it, I read it and said, 'I'm going to do that on Johnny Carson one day. And he's going to love it. And he's going to invite me to sit on the couch.' I knew it was more than funny, I knew it was classic. And it saved me."

The routine is indeed a classic, beginning with

her phoning the Almighty to find out why fleas are here. She gets Him on the phone, but He puts her on hold ("Somebody's at the gate"), and she sings along with "Onward Christian Soldiers" ("It's *not* a tape?" she says. They're *good!*"). When God comes back, He starts to tell her why He created Charo, and Ellen says, Jesus Christ, that's *not* why she called. (She apologizes for the slip, telling Him that Jesus was actually a good idea. "We're still talkin' about *that*," she assures Him.)

In answer to her question, God tells Ellen that He created fleas so that people could be gainfully employed by the flea-collar and bug-spray industries. She has to admit that that makes sense, and after God sneezes ("Bless yourself!" Ellen says), He tells her some really bad knock-knock jokes; of course, Ellen has to laugh at them ("Knock-knock. Who's There? God. God who? Godzilla"), though she finally finds the nerve to tell God she's got to run.

Though the format of the bit is reminiscent of Bob Newhart's brilliant watchman at the Empire State Building who calls for instructions when King Kong shows up, the blend of irreverence and compassion is pure Ellen.

After several months back at Clyde's, her spirits still low—though no one in the audience would have known it—Ellen learned that the TV cable service Showtime was sponsoring a contest to find the "Funniest Person in America." All anyone had to do to enter was send in a videotape of their performance.

Ellen did.

Much to her surprise, she became a finalist, and then she and the other finalists did their routines on a Showtime special.

Ellen won.

She says with justifiable amazement, "In one year, I went from making coffee for lawyers to being the Funniest Person in America." She adds, though, "It was nice to win, but imagine having to wear a title like that around your neck for a year." She knew that every audience in the country would have a large contingent of people who would fold their arms across their chests and scowl. *"Show me,"* they'd say. Some audiences would even have Marines.

But with the national exposure the contest gave her, as both an albatross and a door-opener, Ellen knew that it was time to take her act on the road.

Using the money she'd managed to save, she bought a Winnebago, attached a large nose above the front bumper ("Big noses are funny," Ellen explains), and set out to try and parlay her victory —and hopes—into a real live career.

As it happens, Ellen wasn't the only one making changes in her life.

10

Reopen That Golden Gate

Is a life in comedy always fun? No. But is anything always anything?

—Albert Brooks

Ellen's mother was prouder than she'd ever been when Ellen won the Showtime contest, even though she saw some immediate pitfalls.

First, she was worried about Ellen touring the country and its comedy clubs on her own. The nutty Winnebago alone was sure to call attention to her, and maybe attract kooks or the police.

She was also more than a little concerned that Ellen would be working without an agent and booking herself into bars and potentially seedy clubs, with no guarantee that she would be safe from drunk or rowdy patrons, or that she'd be paid by unscrupulous owners.

Privately, Betty wished that she could be with

Ellen, keeping her company on the road and doing her bookkeeping work for her.

Betty was also deeply concerned for Ellen's safety when she *wasn't* on the road. She was convinced that living with other young women in a not-terribly-secure building in a big city like San Francisco wasn't the greatest idea in the world. Moreover, Ellen enjoyed the city's nightlife and would be coming in late many nights, often driving or walking alone.

But Betty had several crises of her own to deal with, and while she was preoccupied with her daughter's well-being, Ellen was also worrying about herself.

First, shortly after Ellen moved to San Francisco and took to the road, her mother went into the hospital for major surgery.

Ellen was in a panic. She couldn't rearrange all her dates to be with her mother, though, fortunately, Betty's mother was able to come up from New Orleans. While Grandma sat by Betty's bedside night and day until she was fully recovered, Ellen felt miserable and terribly guilty that she wasn't able to be there. She phoned several times a day and sent flowers every time she passed a flower shop.

Second, and ultimately more upsetting to Betty, her marriage to Roy came to an end.

At the same time that Ellen moved to San Francisco, Betty and Roy had moved one hundred miles southwest of Atlanta, to Tyler, Texas. With

Ellen even farther from her than before, and away from her dear friend Jimmy, Betty felt more alone than ever. She had never felt as close to Roy as she'd hoped, and now that sense of isolation was even worse. This estrangement heightened the realization that she simply had to make something of the second half of her life—she had to do something that would benefit her daughter or others, not to mention herself.

After getting a separation from Roy, Betty went to New Orleans and attended school to become a speech therapist. She wasn't sure that that was how she wanted to spend her life; but for now, at least, it was something she knew she'd enjoy and could feel proud doing.

As it turned out, Betty didn't have to worry about Ellen being unsafe in San Francisco: Ellen was rarely there for very long. While San Francisco was her home base, and while she played all the comedy clubs there whenever she was in town, it wasn't really home.

A mutual friend offered to introduce her to Budd Friedman, the monocled, Los Angeles–based comedy impresario who had founded the famed Improv clubs (and is best known to the public as the host of A & E's *Evening at the Improv* on cable). Ellen went down to see him and says, "I auditioned, and he gave me some great spots. Instead of having to wait around for hours like the rest of the beginning comics, he had me booked into the good time slots."

The importance of the gig can't be understated, as it was common for agents, talent scouts, directors, and producers to come to the Improv looking for new talent. And working with Jay Leno there one night turned out to be vitally important to Ellen's future.

Thereafter, if she wasn't crashing with her friend in Los Angeles and performing at the Improv, she was constantly on the road, traveling an average of three hundred days a year. It was exhausting and disorienting. She made it a habit of greeting the audience by name ("Hi, Littleton! How ya doin' tonight, Muncie?"), but there were nights when the name literally slipped from her mind. She managed to turn that into a joke ("Hi, Moscow!"), though she found it frustrating.

Still, it was a good life, better than anything Ellen had known in her twenty-five years.

Yet even at this point in her career, with only two years of stand-up behind her, Ellen had come to the conclusion that "It's kind of a weird profession. You sit alone all day in a hotel in a strange city. But as soon as I walk onstage and hear and feel people responding to me, there's no profession like it." She adds, "There is no greater feeling than to see a thought, a tiny idea, transform into a story onstage in Minneapolis and two thousand people laughing."

She told one interviewer that apart from coming up with funny, fresh material, one of the greatest challenges to her is that you have to "self-start. It's my job. I can't just go to work and sit behind a desk and type. I've got all those people out there looking at me."

Fortunately, getting out of New Orleans had provided her with new fodder for the comedy mill. (Along with new recreations: As she later told *Entertainment Tonight*, whenever she checks into a nice hotel, she stands on the bed and starts bouncing. "I don't know why," she admitted, but she does it just the same.)

Two of her best-known bits came from travel and being away from those near and dear to her.

The first has to do with airplanes. With variations, it generally goes like this:

"Whatever the problem, you ever notice that whatever you ask the stewardess, the answer is going to be 'club soda.' You know that.

" 'Excuse me, I have the hiccups. Could you—'

" 'Club soda will get that. Be right back.'

" 'I spilled a little red sauce on my pants—'

" 'Club soda will get that, be right back.'

" 'The wing is on fire.'

" 'Club soda will get that, be right back.'

"Her job is to bring us the food: six peanuts in this little tiny package, and we get very upset if we don't get it.

" *'I didn't get my peanuts!'*

" 'You gonna eat yours? We're diggin' our finger around in it.' Anywhere else, anyone offers that to us, it's, 'I don't want that, get that away from me. . . . Six peanuts!' But on the plane, we *need* that.

"And if we're on a long enough flight, if we're lucky enough to get real food, who's cooking this food, midget chefs? Tiny little portions, tiny little salads and salad dressings in these containers. Immediately, when you open it, it's on your neighbor's lap. You're, 'I'm very sorry. Can I just dip my lettuce? That's all I have.'"

The second truly classic routine came from the mail she receives:

"Friends will write me letters, they run out of room on the front of the letter, they write 'over' on the bottom of the letter. Like I'm that much of a moron. Like I need that there. Because if it wasn't there, I'd get to the bottom of the page:

"'And so Kathy and I went shopping and we—'

"That's the craziest thing! I don't know why she just ended it that way. I hope nothin' happened to her. She managed to seal the envelope. It's a good thing some of these letters have the arrow to show you where the back of the page *is*. Because you don't know. Could it be—*this way?*

"It's on the back! Don't call her, I found it."

Along with wide exposure came critical attention, almost all of it favorable. *Esquire* praised her "sweetly expressed mistrust of everything" and her "penchant for anxious free association," citing the time she was talking about mud baths and the uniquely Californian idea that going naked around strangers is the best way to relax. When someone in the audience volunteered that she herself had done this, Ellen said without missing a beat, "Did you have to get on the goat and sing the theme from *Shaft?*"

The New York Times praised Ellen for her "off-beat story-telling, strategic pauses, and dramatic facial expressions that remind some people of Bob Newhart." They were particularly impressed with her phone call to God and the saga of her folks not liking her and selling her to Iroquois Indians.

In her book *Stand-Up Comedy,* comedian Judy Carter called Ellen a master of "the callback," where reference is made to something the stand-up said previously.

Carter points to this part of Ellen's act as a standout use of the form:

"Dogs hate it when you blow in their face. I'll tell you who really hates that—my grandmother. Which is odd, because when we're driving she really loves to hang her head out the window."

Later in her act, Ellen says, "I think everybody has a philosophical side to them. I grew up that way because of my grandmother. At a very young age she said to me, 'Life is like a blender. You have so many different speeds, you have mix, blend, stir, puree, and you never use them all. In life you have so many different abilities and you never use them all.

"I said, 'Grandma—' and then I just blew in her face. . . . I really don't like her."

(That's not true, of course: Ellen uses her grandmother so much *because* she adores her. And like

Buddy Morra said, you serve the audience best by giving them "what *you* want.")

Other critics, not to mention audiences, were also smitten with Ellen's one-liners and uncanny observations. Among these is the bit about her family running a petting zoo. "And then a heavy petting zoo for people who *really* liked the animals just a whole lot."

Describing the mating habits of golden eagles, she talks about how they connect while flying at eighty miles an hour, three or four miles up. "And then they start dropping, and they don't stop dropping until the act is completed. So it's not uncommon that they both fall all the way to the ground, hit the ground, both of them die. That's how committed they are to this. I thought to myself, 'Boy, don't we feel like wimps for stopping to answer the phone.'"

She goes on to say, "I don't know about you, but if I'm one of these two birds, you're getting close to the ground . . . I would seriously consider fakin' it."

Her cat Ethel is an indoor cat, "but somehow she is sneakin' out at night. 'Cause the other morning I found a stamp on her paw. . . . I wouldn't have noticed myself, but I just bought this new black light and she passed right under it and I said, 'Hey, what's that on your paw?'"

* * *

"I'm a godmother. That's a great thing, to be a godmother. She calls me 'God' for short; that's cute. I taught her that."

"Penguins mate for life. Which doesn't really surprise me that much. 'Cause they all look exactly alike. It's not like they're gonna meet a better-looking penguin someday."

"I ask people why they have deer heads on their walls. They always say because it's such a beautiful animal. There you go. I think my mother's attractive, but I have photographs of her."

Then she plays the part of the hunter, boasting about how she bagged the animal, and acts out how it would be if it really *were* her mother's head on the wall. She points out that her mother had nice legs too—and they're in the next room, should anyone want to see them.

Ellen suggests that the heads we should really have on the wall are those of people who deserve to be there, like burglars.

She adds the deers she feels most sorry for "are the ones that you see on the walls of bars or restaurants. They have the silly party hats on 'em, the silly sunglasses and streamers hanging from their necks. Obviously they were at a party, havin' a good time. They don't know. They're in there dancin', enjoyin' themselves. . . . 'Hey, who invited the guy in the orange vest?'"

* * *

"It's so weird all the different names they have for groups of animals. They have pride of lions, school of fish, rack of lamb. . . ."

"Eclectic" doesn't begin to describe Ellen's act. Even Ellen is loathe to describe it: "I couldn't," she says. "I don't want to be able to be compared to anyone else, because I want to be me, not a version of someone else."

She also points out an irony of having become a stand-up: The more time she spends working on her comedy, the more serious she's become in her day-to-day life.

Whereas quips used to fly among friends and co-workers, she now says she's only funny "when I have to be. And when I feel like it. Or if someone is crying, like if someone falls down or some authority figure is telling me what to do."

Like any hobby that becomes a vocation, being funny, to Ellen, is no laughing matter.

11

Heeeeere's Ellen

*I hate television, I hate it as much as peanuts.
But I can't stop eating peanuts.*

—Orson Welles

Ellen made sure she was back in San Francisco to compete in the prestigious San Francisco Comedy Festival. She finished second behind Sinbad, though he says it's a distinction that has very little meaning.

"I think it's crazy that people feel this need to pick a 'best' at these things," he says during a break while taping his own HBO special. "'Cause I mean, I'm not better than Ellen DeGeneres and she's not better than Richard Jeni or Bobby Slayton or anything like that. We're different, that's all. I remember one of these things where Eddie Murphy finished second or third behind I don't even *remember* who. It's nuts.

"You can see that coming in second didn't hurt Ellen, though. It wasn't like when they were casting her show they went, 'Well, let's see, man. Should we star her . . . or that guy who won the San Francisco Comedy Festival?'"

Sinbad's right. In any case, more important than who won was the fact that the Festival brought Ellen to the attention of manager Buddy Morra, who carries a great deal of weight in the comedy world.

Ellen says, "He's the manager of people like Robin Williams and Billy Crystal, so he got the talent coordinator of *The Tonight Show,* Jim McCauley, to come see me. I had opened for Jay [Leno] at the Improv, so Jay sat Jim McCauley down, and Jim was between Jay and Buddy Morra, watching me." She says that with her cheering section on either side, McCauley "never had a chance."

When she finished her set, the trio went over to Ellen to congratulate her, and McCauley invited her to make her debut on *The Tonight Show* with Johnny Carson.

Ellen has said that if she could have bottled and sold what she felt at that moment, she'd have been the wealthiest person on Earth.

At that time, *The Tonight Show* was the mecca for any stand-up, an appearance virtually guaranteeing invitations to other shows and big bookings nationwide. However, that wasn't what Ellen was thinking at the time. She already had those things. What she wanted was what she had promised herself nearly five years before.

Ellen went on the show and did her Phone Call to God, knowing that not once in Johnny's twenty-four-year reign had a female stand-up ever finished her routine and been asked to join Johnny on the couch. Those things were never rehearsed: If an entertainer pleased the King of Late Night, he motioned them over. If not, it was a quick cut to Johnny applauding and then to a commercial.

When Ellen finished, she took a quick bow and then looked over at Johnny to see his reaction. He was smiling and clapping. That's it.

She started to look away, and then she saw him crook his finger and motion her over. As she headed toward the sofa, she experienced a rush of emotion as the memory of the years of indecision, the pain of writing the piece, the long and friendless nights on the road all washed over her. She had come through it all and reached the spot she had promised she'd get to.

Ellen did five more *Tonight Show* appearances before Johnny Carson retired, and she continued to appear after her good friend Jay Leno took over. It was the first spot, however, that helped to launch her TV career. As much as she was constantly in demand on the road, Ellen quickly became a hit on cable and on various TV specials. Most notably, she was on *The Young Comedians All-Star Reunion* in 1986, was one of the four featured stand-ups (along with Paula Poundstone, Judy Tenuta, and Rita Rudner) on *Women of the Night* in 1987, and costarred on *The Comedy Club Special* in 1988.

All of which brought her a good income and satisfaction, but not exactly household celebrity. Once, while stopping at an ABC radio station to promote a show, she went up to the desk and announced herself to the receptionist.

"You're not on the list," she was informed rather curtly. The receptionist called the interviewer. "Your guest is here for three-thirty. Miss Generis."

Ellen corrected her. "DeGENeres."

The woman said, "Miss DEEgenAIRres."

Ellen corrected her once more. This time the receptionist got it right.

Ellen adored San Francisco.

She loved the culture, she thrived on the nightlife, she enjoyed the sights. (While strolling along the famed Fisherman's Wharf, she once saw a couple of gulls picking apart a lobster. Stopping to watch them, she wondered aloud, "How'd they get ahold of cash like that? Because lobsters have got to be about fourteen bucks.")

After living in the Bay City for two years, however, she decided to try and cut down on the number of days she traveled. The only way to do this without losing her audience—or her income—was to get on TV or in the movies, not necessarily as a stand-up but as an actress.

"I'm not Meryl Streep," Ellen has said, but she knew she'd get work if she were down there, free to attend auditions.

So in 1985 she moved to Los Angeles to be where the action was.

At the same time, her mother, Betty, was also at a crossroads. She had returned to Tyler and to Roy, unhappy with her life, with the sameness of each day. The focus of her love, and perhaps her own unfulfilled ambitions, was her daughter. When Ellen moved to Southern California, Betty decided she belonged at her side. Finally divorcing Roy, she moved to Los Angeles to do what she had wanted to do all those years in Atlanta: help Ellen manage her career.

12

Comedy Tonight

The other day I bought a wastebasket and carried it home in a paper bag. And when I got home I put the paper bag in the wastebasket.

—Lily Tomlin

Television is a lot like that, now more than ever.

Stand-up comedians help network TV earn big profits by bringing their skilled comic timing and proven characters to peoples' homes and hauling in huge ratings. Unfortunately, television invariably rewards comics by stuffing them in the wastebasket, stifling stand-ups by starring them in formulaic programs, situation comedies that are designed to appeal to the widest possible audience—which usually isn't synonymous with quality.

Late stand-up Andy Kaufman, who starred on *Taxi*, used to say that "TV stands for tunnel vision, and that's on a good day. An extremely good day. The rest of the time it's terrible, very." Richard Pryor once complained of *his* ill-fated variety show that NBC "retained about six thousand people to do nothing but mess with my material." Appropriately enough, when Pryor dared to appear on his show in a skin-colored leotard and bitched that he'd been emasculated, the censors cut the segment.

However tense it becomes, though, the dance between the networks and the stand-ups goes on.

"Of course it does," says writer and producer Linda Bloodworth-Thomason, creator of *Designing Women* and *Woman of the House* and one of the few really good writers working in network TV. "What stand-up or actor wouldn't want forty million pairs of eyes on them in a single night? And what writer wouldn't want the advantage of knowing ahead of time the strengths and weaknesses of their comic performer?"

It's not surprising that stand-ups have been a staple of television since the dawn of the medium. They were always extremely popular on radio, and as early as June of 1948, when there were as yet just a few hundred thousand sets in homes across the United States, NBC took a chance and hired a moderately successful stage, screen, and radio comedian named Milton Berle to host the new vaudeville-style *Texaco Star Theater*, later called *The Milton Berle Show*. (Bigger stars didn't want to be a part of the medium. Not yet.)

Berle was a funny, wonderfully lowbrow host, telling old jokes, dressing in drag, and exchanging predictable barbs with guests. But he dominated Tuesday nights for eight years, and in its first two seasons his show was the driving force behind the sale of nearly six million sets. (Comedian Joe E. Lewis once quipped, "Milton Berle is responsible for selling millions and millions of sets. I know this is true because when Berle was on, I sold mine, my uncle sold his, my aunt sold hers. . . .")

Networks drew on the ranks of stand-ups to host other shows, and half-hour sitcoms proliferated the year after Berle debuted. Some of them, like *The Goldbergs,* were transplants from radio, and some of them were created expressly for the new medium, like *I Love Lucy.* But virtually every season for the next thirty years, the networks created sitcoms and variety shows to showcase the talents of seasoned stand-ups. With varying degrees of success, the small screen was home to the likes of George Burns and Gracie Allen, the Smothers Brothers, Phyllis Diller, Lily Tomlin (on Rowan and Martin's *Laugh-In*), Buddy Hackett, Bob Newhart, Flip Wilson, Bill Cosby, Jonathan Winters, Robin Williams, Freddie Prinze, Redd Foxx, Billy Crystal, Gabe Kaplan, and many others.

The wildfire growth of cable in the 1980s continued TV's love affair with stand-ups, many of whom starred in HBO or Showtime specials, which allowed them to do their stage acts live and unexpurgated. Ellen was certainly no stranger to cable: In addition to her immediate post–*Tonight Show* gigs, she had her own HBO *One Night Stand* in 1989. Cable proved to be *the* breeding grounds for hot new talent, and the networks watched the ratings—then raided the cable rosters for new stars to headline their own sitcoms. The comedians answered the call, despite the fact that working in Hollywood is a painful experience, one that Robin Williams once likened to "being a hemophiliac in a razor factory."

The biggest hit to feature a stand-up transplanted from cable was *Roseanne,* which debuted in October of 1988 starring Roseanne Barr, the self-proclaimed "domestic goddess" of a handful of cable specials. She was unpolished, she was unsophisticated, but she seemed to speak to every woman in America who felt as she did: "The way I look at it, if the kids are alive when my husband comes home from work, then I've done my job." (Compare that to the cheerful simplicity of what Gracie Allen had said forty years before: "A woman came to ask the doctor if a woman should have children after thirty-five. I said, 'Thirty-five children is enough for any woman!'")

The cable-to-network trend hit a disappointing rough spot when popular Richard Lewis (along with Jamie Lee Curtis) bombed in the sophisticated *Anything But Love* the following year (Lewis crashed and burned again, this time with fellow stand-up Don Rickles, in the fall of 1993 with *Daddy Dearest*) and when *Seinfeld,* starring hot stand-up Jerry Seinfeld, debuted to so-so ratings in May of the following year.

But NBC had faith in Seinfeld and stuck with his show, and the audience soon found it. Then Tuesday nights caught fire in the fall of 1991 when Tim Allen debuted in *Home Improvement,* Paul Reiser appeared in the hit *Mad About You* in 1992, and Brett Butler was a smash in *Grace Under Fire* in 1993. Though the disastrous *Paula Poundstone Show* was gone lickety-split from the ABC fall lineup that same year, it didn't daunt the network in its quest for the next Tim or Brett.

Unlike many other stand-ups, Ellen never thought she'd be a TV star. She thought she might get "best friend" or character parts in movies, but she didn't see how her laid-back style and that "offbeat story-telling" of hers would translate to a weekly sitcom.

She used to joke that she was so *not* leading actor material, in fact, that casting directors never quite knew what to make of her. When she went on auditions, she says, it was "usually more like me and Gary Coleman."

The truth of the matter is that Ellen *was* offered parts, and she actually got recurring roles on two different shows. But she wasn't happy with the results, and after the second flop—by far the bigger and more visible of the two—she resolved to hold out for something she believed in.

"I'm pretty picky," she told *Parade*. She was also earning a hefty six-figure income from stand-up and didn't see any reason to go on TV and appear in something unsatisfactory just to make seven figures. Quality was more important to her than a bigger house, than appealing to what she called "the lowest common denominator. I like taking you on the whole ride." In other words, giving an audience her all.

The two series on which she'd already costarred gave her little hope that the medium could accommodate her.

Ellen's first regular series was *Open House,* a half-hour comedy that debuted on Fox in August of 1989. A spinoff from the far superior but low-rated sitcom *Duet, Open House* was about pushy young realtor Linda Phillips (Alison LaPlaca) who worked for Juan Verde Real Estate, where she tried to outsell equally pushy Ted Nichols (Philip Charles MacKenzie). Ellen was featured as Margo Van Meter, the barely competent, man-hungry receptionist who spent most of her time lusting after her boss, Roger McSwain (Nick Tate). *Open House* was closed down and off the air by July of 1990.

Her second series was the highly anticipated *Laurie Hill,* the brainchild of Carol Black and Neal Marlens, the creators of the wildly successful *The Wonder Years. Laurie Hill,* which aired on ABC in the nine-thirty time slot on Wednesday nights, was a mostly serious look at working mother/doctor Laurie Hill (DeLane Mathews), who is both a career woman and the parent of five-year-old son, Leo (Eric Lloyd).

Dubbing the series "The Blunder Years," *TV Guide* observed that no one was going to want to watch a show about people who were as unhappy as the Hills. However, they did say that Ellen, as nurse

Nancy MacIntyre, "provide[d] desperately needed comic relief—and not enough of it."

Ellen's opinion of *Laurie Hill* was even lower, if that's possible: "I thought maybe they [Black and Marlens] would see something in me and start writing for me but the show was just about Laurie Hill. I think in the pilot I maybe had two lines. It was very frustrating.

"I had so little to do it was almost ridiculous. I was praying for it to get canceled."

She got her wish. The show was canned after just a few weeks.

Thereafter, what was offered was either mediocre or just not right for her, mostly more supporting roles in unexciting comedies. Most recently, in the summer of 1993, she was in the running for the lead role in *Café Americain,* an NBC series about an American divorcée who goes to Paris and gets a job at a popular bistro.

Ellen's enthusiasm for *Café Americain* was anything but high, and she was actually relieved when the part went to Valerie Bertinelli. That proved to be lucky for Ellen, as the show was a bomb.

13

ABCDeGeneres

Television is now so desperately hungry for material that they're scraping the top of the barrel.

—Gore Vidal

After licking their wounds and regrouping following the painful demise of *Laurie Hill*, Black and Marlens took a look around. Despite the fact that Ellen had been associated with the project—being an actor on a TV failure usually means professional death or at least a several-year moratorium—the producers were quite high on Ellen.

The producers felt that she had an appealing TV persona, and they were keenly aware that stand-ups were attracting a wide audience as TV stars. Equally important, they had a commitment from the Walt Disney Studios' Touchstone Television division to create a new series. The duo asked Ellen what she thought about getting back in the saddle with them, about letting them develop a sitcom around her.

Ellen was torn. She didn't like the process of trying to fit herself into someone else's half-hour sitcom concept, that much was certain. She also had a very clear vision of what she was about, of what her comedy was about, and the kinds of situations that inspired it. Unlike many stand-ups, Ellen had never had other people writing jokes for her, and she wasn't sure how comfortable she'd feel starring in a show, even playing someone like herself, with other people writing the material.

But it *was* a sitcom of her own, and that carried a lot of weight.

Naturally, there was only one way to find out if it would or wouldn't work. And the producers presented it to her in such a way that made it seem do-able. Black and Marlens agreed to let Ellen look over their shoulders as they worked, to allow her to contribute her thoughts along the way—as few or as many as she liked. The producers didn't necessarily have to incorporate them, but they assured Ellen that if the finished script were not to her liking, she didn't have to shoot it. The brake, if not the entire process, was hers to control, and she apparently had nothing to lose by allowing the process to go forward.

Or did she? There *was* a downside.

Once you board the train, it tends to build a momentum of its own. Actors end up compromising a little here, a little there, and it turns out to be a lot before they're through—especially when it comes to accepting the conventions that govern prime-time network shows: the sometimes awkward breaks for commercials, the idiotic laugh tracks (which are used to "sweeten" the often nonexistent studio laughter), and the reluctance to address controversial issues or use surreal images (like Grandma sticking her head out the window), elements that are often the meat of a stand-up's act. It took years before Roseanne Arnold had the clout to address birth control or have the "lesbian kiss" on her show, and the successful but risqué *NYPD Blue* still isn't shown by certain affiliates.

But the stars *do* get seduced by the attention, by rubbing shoulders with other stars, by the excitement and ego boost of having yes-people all around them, and their faces in homes nationwide. Even well-intentioned comedians like Ellen can, and do—and will—get waylaid.

And there's something else that happens when a potential star rolls the sitcom dice: She or he has to make sure they're getting together with the right producers. Before any network buys a show, they put close to a million dollars on the table and commission a single episode, a pilot. This way they can see how the idea works, how the actors mesh, and whether the star has any charisma before committing tens of millions of dollars *and* a time slot to the show.

If an actor shoots a pilot and it stinks, the smell has a way of permeating all four networks. If a pilot starring Ellen turned out to be a loser, she'd find it difficult getting herself another pilot for seasons to come.

Were Black and Marlens the "right" producers?

Would they be energized or hamstrung by the disaster of *Laurie Hill?* Would the network be leery because of that show's failure, would it color their view of her sitcom?

In the end, Ellen just told herself to do it. There was no reason anything should go seriously wrong, not if she monitored every step of the process and refused to be seduced by the money—which might prove the most difficult thing of all, since the sums could be considerable. A relatively unknown star of a new sitcom can make a minimum of $35,000 a week for the first season, which could more than double by the second if the show's a hit. Then there are the tens of millions of dollars that pour in if there are enough episodes to sell to syndication— at least three seasons' worth. And for a stand-up comic, there is an added bonus: going back on the road, playing to sold-out houses, signing the inevitable movie deal, and setting up a production company to produce shows for other actors.

Not bad for someone who didn't know what to do with herself just a few years before.

And there was another thing to consider.

Once-welcomed TV faces tend to grow tired over three, four, or five years, and audiences who once embraced Candice Bergen as vibrant and feisty, or Roseanne as refreshingly blunt, or who found newcomer Brett Butler of *Grace Under Fire* a little too mellow for their tastes, might take a liking to sunshiny, well-meaning, slightly off-center, and fumbling Ellen Morgan.

Ellen decided to go forward. She wanted to be on

TV, and unless it were a total, embarrassing disaster, she told herself that she could go back to stand-up, regroup, and try movies again, or even write books like Rita Rudner and Louie Anderson were doing.

Early in the spring of 1993, Ellen signed a deal with Black/Marlens Productions. Despite her reservations, she was excited at the prospect of brainstorming and building a new show.

14
Step by Step

Have you noticed that TV families never watch television?

—Henny Youngman

TV Guide first referred to *These Friends of Mine* in its "Series in the Wings" column in September of 1993. Describing it as *"Seinfeld* in skirts," the magazine said the show was about "three female yuppies who complain about things like dates and driver's-license photos. Oh, yes—to add the Elaine factor, there's also a guy on hand."

That was neither fair nor accurate. As Ellen later said, "On his show, Jerry is the more or less normal one and there are all these colorful characters around him. On my show, I'm the person who always trips."

The truth is, long before there even *was* a *Seinfeld,* or before they had Ellen on their side, Black and Marlens had had the various ideas that would comprise *These Friends of Mine.*

Like all producers, the two had files filled with

notes and concepts. Among these were ideas about a single woman living with a platonic male friend; two young girlfriends with radically different personalities; and an eager-to-please non-career woman who goes from job to job. However, they stopped developing all of these ideas when they switched over to *Laurie Hill*.

When that series took a very early nosedive, Black and Marlens struck their deal with Ellen and then immediately added another person to their creative team to brainstorm and develop the ideas into a concept that would accommodate Ellen's talent: sharp, recent University of Pennsylvania graduate David Rosenthal, a writer and colleague from *Laurie Hill*.

The process of coming up with the TV show isn't, however, as simple as fitting a comic into a concept. This is especially true where women are concerned. Pat Richardson, the costar of *Home Improvement*, says that there's a problem all women face when they go onto TV: breaking free of stereotypes.

"I and many actresses feel so angry in so many ways about the way that things have been going down on TV," she says. "I think that television is incredibly powerful and influential, and drama and comedy can both offer a potent examination of masculinism meets feminism. But it can't be one running roughshod over the other, or crashing into it and getting nowhere the way it is on a show like *Married . . . With Children,* where she's a total bitch and he's a complete idiot. Both people have to have a valid point of view.

"The problem is, when women try to be serious on TV comedy, like Murphy Brown and Roseanne, women tend to love it while men, including critics, just say they're being crabby, not serious."

Her costar Tim Allen agrees. *"Of course* men and women relate to TV differently," he says. "They *watch* TV differently. Women are looking to connect, for relationships and story. Men are just looking for explosions, car chases, fire, and breasts. Instant thrills. I'm not a sociologist, and I don't know when and if that'll ever change. But that's definitely the way things are now."

The creative trio working for and with Ellen had no intention of breaking new ground. What they wanted to do was have a hit after the debacle of *Laurie Hill.* Nor were they interested in presenting a dysfunctional Bundy-type family. They wanted to go for laughs the same way Ellen did onstage, with wry observations rather than deep social commentary.

They knew that they had to start with the typical sitcom "home base"—that is, give Ellen someone to continually talk to and play off of. At the same time, they had to keep up a steady flow of new characters to trigger what they described, in one early summary of the show, as Ellen's "humorous musings [that] celebrate the mundane moments of life—with a twist."

One of the first ideas they kicked around was something along the lines of *The Mary Tyler Moore Show,* with Ellen living alone and hanging out with a sympathetic but quirky girlfriend-neighbor like Rhoda. The neighbor evolved into the character of Holly, whom they decided would be a friend of Ellen's from high school. That would give the writers someone who could remind Ellen of some of the bonehead things she'd done in the past.

The concept of having Ellen live alone didn't seem quite cutting edge enough, though, and they didn't like the notion of moving Holly in with Ellen. That would have evolved into tit-for-tat humor like *Laverne and Shirley* or *The Odd Couple,* which just wasn't Ellen. However, the idea of having a male best friend as a roommate was fresh and much more appealing, especially if the two were not sexually involved with one another. Without that tension and flirtation, the differences between men and women could be explored in an open and honest way.

The roommate became Adam, who ended up taking more ribs from Ellen than he gave.

When it was decided that Ellen, Holly, and Adam would all be relatively sane, albeit with the flaws of naiveté and gullibility (the viewer has to feel just a *bit* smarter), the creators added a wilder friend, Anita, to serve as an occasional spark plug.

After considering various kinds of jobs for Ellen, including a complaint department and travel agency, the creators toyed with a coffeeshop setting— upscale, an espresso bar, not the diner from *Alice.* The creators felt that in that kind of setting they could do a strong ensemble show like *Cheers,* only without the alcohol. The "friends" would gather there, and Ellen could play a role like either Ted Danson or Kirstie Alley had on *Cheers.*

The whole thing sounded too much like *Cheers,* however, so the creators altered that to a combination bookstore and coffee bar where Ellen was just an employee: That would not only give her the steady stream of new faces as a source of comedy, but she could comment on trendy new book titles, work on creating unusual displays, and play off of her boss, Susan, and a co-worker, Joe. These characters were conceived as terminally cranky and a bit dizzy, respectively.

Several titles were considered for the show, including *The Ellen DeGeneres Show* and simply *Ellen.* However, in order to emphasize the ensemble nature of the program, they decided to go with something a little more well-defined: *These Friends of Mine.*

At first, Ellen wasn't crazy about it: She felt that viewers would relate to a person, like they did to Roseanne or Seinfeld, better than they would to a concept. But after *Laurie Hill,* Black and Marlens wanted to stay away from "names" and to be as clear as possible about what the show was. Besides, *The Wonder Years* had been an enduring hit for them, and *Home Improvement,* which said it all, was the biggest hit on TV.

When everyone was more or less agreed on the title and on the key elements, Black, Marlens, and Rosenthal sat down and wrote a script with Ellen's input. When they were finished, they got the finished teleplay over to Ellen.

Ellen read the script at home, in one sitting. Her initial response was positive, and she read through it again. One of the keys to judging comedy is if you start to laugh, *anticipating* a joke you've already heard.

She did.

Once she'd had a chance to digest the material, Ellen began to have a *great* feeling about the show and its potential.

Ellen told *The New York Times*, "I was laughing out loud when I read the script. I knew what I could do with it." She said that what struck her right away about what Black, Marlens, and Rosenthal had done was that they'd captured perfectly what it was like "being single and trying to figure out things in life the hard way." As she described the show to *Mademoiselle*, it's about that "inbetween" stage when "you're just finished with the cinder block and plank bookshelves, but you're not married yet." And as she told *The New York Post*, she loved the fact that her character is "this person who's desperate to make everyone happy. Unfortunately, when she does that, she ends up putting her foot in her mouth." She felt the comedy potential in a situation like that was extremely rich.

She phoned the creators, telling them that she would do the show, and the script went off to Touchstone and ABC. The studio and network gave their okays, and by the late winter of 1993 the team was making preparations to shoot the half-hour pilot.

Ellen told *Us* magazine that although the scripts were being written by others, the basis for *These Friends of Mine* is "how I look at life. So it's my take on being in line at the supermarket behind someone with way too many items to be in the express lane. . . . It's just about life. Stuff we can all do and relate to, with my spin on it, which usually means it spins way out of control. It's about trying to fit in but not quite making it, and not caring because I'm not sure I want to."

However, she made it clear that what she was going to do on the show *was* acting. She wasn't just going to get onto the soundstage and be Ellen DeGeneres.

"I think the character I play is a lot more naive and a little more gullible. She tries so hard, but she's always getting into trouble. It's a little like *Lucy.*

"I would like to think that my life's not like that."

Ellen said that if she had to characterize her new sitcom, it wasn't comparable to *Seinfeld* or *The Mary Tyler Moore Show.* Rather, she viewed *These Friends of Mine* as "a smarter, hipper version of *I Love Lucy,*" albeit one that didn't go "so far that I'm in a man's suit with a mustache trying to fool Ricky that I'm not his wife."

While that statement may come across as a bit arrogant—Lucy is a legend and Ellen is still Ellen

—the point the comedian was trying to make is a valid one: She wanted to do a show that was funny while at the same time staying true to the kinds of things viewers might be thinking, facing, and feeling. A show, as she put it, "that everybody talks about the next day."

15
Networking

Humor is emotional chaos remembered in tranquillity.

—James Thurber

Comedian Sinbad had a very successful stand-up career and a moderately successful movie career going when he decided to star in his own sitcom, *The Sinbad Show,* in the fall of 1993. His reasons, he said, had nothing to do with greed or ego.

"We crave entertainment in America," he says, "because, man, when you got a bad job, you're living a bad life and you're just bored. When you watch a show, well, it takes you to another place. I love TV, man."

When a stand-up moves into situation comedy, however, the transition isn't always a smooth one. Just because someone can tell jokes or stories from a stage and has good comic timing, that's no guarantee they can act.

Stand-ups who do "characters" onstage usually have the easiest time making the switch to acting:

Consider Richard Pryor, Billy Crystal, and of course Academy Award–winning Whoopi Goldberg. Stand-ups who are more or less themselves onstage find it considerably more difficult to be anything else: Witness Roseanne Arnold and Richard Lewis.

The jury is still out on Tim Allen, who says that he is learning fast from his costars and that it isn't necessarily a one-way street.

"Sometimes they surprise me, as I do them," he says. "Because I'm not a professional actor, and I need an audience, if I start getting flat someone'll come up with a trick to goose me. They do this to me all the time—say something that'll piss me off. I'll get testy and say, 'That's not in the script,' and the director'll say, 'Now *that's* the attitude I want.'

"But on the other hand, these are actors who haven't really practiced the craft of comedy. The funny stuff comes very naturally to me. I mean, I can just do facial expressions and get laughs. Or dialogue that we don't think is particularly funny when we read it—when I do it, it's funny. I don't say that to be conceited, but because that's what I've been doing for nineteen years. I can be funny all the time as a result of my training, whereas actors can't.

"Unfortunately," he says ruefully, "I can't do *Death of a Salesman,* or an audience may think that's funny too, even though I'm being very, very serious. It's a tradeoff."

There are many other problems most stand-ups face when going from stage to TV. If her pilot were going to succeed, Ellen had to overcome each of them in a relatively short period of time.

First, stand-ups are accustomed to playing to live audiences, getting what Ellen says is "immediate gratification." Stand-ups feed off this spontaneous reaction, and many thrive on ad-libbing and audience interplay. Though there's an audience for most TV sitcoms, they're in the grandstand, behind the cameras and hanging TV monitors, cut off from the performers. The actors are really playing for the approval of an unseen director in a booth. If a scene doesn't work, they do it again, just as in a movie. Tapings usually start at seven or eight at night and can drag on for hours. Audiences can get worn down, and even veteran performers often lose their edge—especially when the audience stops laughing the fourth time around at jokes that were only so-so the first time.

Second, stand-ups who perform their routines on TV specials or variety shows use the camera differently than they do during the taping of a sitcom. When a stand-up is doing a routine onstage with a camera, most of them tend to treat it as another member of the audience. They don't play to it, but they *do* look at it from time to time. A stand-up will often deliver the setup—the story—to the audience, then hit the camera with the punchline. When a sitcom is shot, the camera is the so-called "fourth wall" of the set. The performers ignore it.

Third, many stand-ups find it difficult and constraining to speak words written by others. This is especially true of words that are churned out by a committee for a weekly show and have to conform to some network executive's idea of what constitutes relatively clean and "acceptable" entertainment. This as opposed to sometimes brutally honest routines that have been thought out over weeks or months, tried out in front of audiences and then fine-tuned and tried out again. As Ellen puts it, "There are many voices involved—from the producers to the studio to the network. With my stand-up, it's me onstage, saying things that I wrote, exactly what I want to say." (Despite her initial enthusiasm for the work of Black, Marlens, and Rosenthal and their writers, Ellen would begin to feel a little edgy about the process as time went on, and changes would be made.)

Fourth, stand-ups are accustomed to working alone onstage. Sharing the spotlight with an ensemble is always a challenge—one that, as it happened, worked even less successfully for Ellen than did the other three.

Conversely, the two big advantages of going from stand-up to sitcom are, as Tim Allen says, that a comic knows how to wring comedy from material, and the star doesn't have to "get to know" the character. Most of the time the producers have simply lifted the persona the stand-up developed for the stage, which allows them to hit the ground running with a fully developed, familiar character. As Garry Shandling puts it on the set of his *Larry Sanders Show,* "It's like slipping on an old mitten. Not an old glove, because I think the networks have the middle finger surgically removed. But the point is, you're comfortable with it."

(However, as actress Annie Potts points out, there's a risk that comes with "playing someone that is too close to themselves, or only playing one kind of role. Any time someone imagines that an actor and the role are the same, the actor has been issued a death sentence. Because then people want to see you like that all the time, and who wants to be *any*thing all the time?")

Making the pilot was a breeze.

Neal Marlens himself was directing the show, and Ellen was slightly nervous as rehearsals got underway. The first day consisted of the read-through, with everyone just sitting around on the set, going over the lines with the writers there to make changes as necessary. Over the next few days they worked out the blocking—with white tape placed on the floor so everyone could hit their marks—and camera movement as the actors weaned themselves off the script. (Sitcoms like Ellen's don't have cue cards for the actors. They have to memorize—and forget—twenty-plus scripts every season.)

Ellen's costars were all experienced, very talented pros who had worked in drama as well as comedy.

Holly Fulger, who was cast as Holly, had been seen most recently as Hollis Amato on *thirtysomething* and as Jamie Lee Curtis's dizzy friend Robin Dulitski on *Anything But Love* (1989–1992). She had also appeared as Carolyn on the TV series *Doctor, Doctor* (1989), was Margie Moodus in *Trenchcoat in Paradise* (1989)—one of several TV movies she's made—and appeared on the big screen as Yvonne in the Tom Selleck film *An Innocent Man* (1989). Her other TV series include *Sable* (1987), in which she played Myke Blackman, and *Jack and Mike* (1986), costarring as Carol Greene.

Arye (pronounced "Ari") Gross made his screen debut in 1984 as Turbo in the little-seen action film *Exterminator II*. His costars were the also soon-to-be-famous Mario Van Peebles and John Turturro. His other films include *Just One of the Guys* (1985), *Soul Man* (1986), *House II: The Second Story* (1987), *The Couch Trip* (1988), *Tequila Sunrise* (1988)—with Mel Gibson, Michelle Pfeiffer, and Kurt Russell—*A Matter of Degrees* (1990), *Coupe De Ville* (1990), *For the Boys* (1990), and *Boris and Natasha* (1992). Though Arye had costarred in the TV movies *Heart of the City* in 1986 and *Confessions: The Two Faces of Evil* in 1994, *These Friends of Mine* was his first series.

Ellen's mother visited the set now and then to provide moral support, her costars were very giving and offered professional support, the producers were there for hand-holding, and reporters were there to make sure, when the time came, that everyone knew the show was coming.

The pilot, which taped on April 15 and 16, 1993, had very modest ambitions. Ellen and her producers wanted to introduce the major "Friends" and let Ellen deliver snippets of the stand-up style of humor she did so well. It didn't want to blaze new trails or shock anyone *too* much; it was cautious. It wanted to be entertaining and endearing but just daring enough so that viewers would come back for a second helping.

The first show didn't introduce the bookstore, Ellen's "tough, hostile" boss Susan (Cristine Rose), or her pompous, portly, Jonathan Winters–like co-worker Joe Farrell (David Higgins, a member of the comedy group the Higgins Boys and Gruber). Instead, it concentrated on Ellen and her platonic, slow-on-the-uptake friend and roomate Adam (Gross)—"We just live together," he tells a Spanish-speaking date in one episode, "No esta intercourse"—and their friends Anita (Maggie Wheeler) and Holly (Fulger).

When the show opens, Ellen and Holly are in line at the Department of Motor Vehicles, Ellen debating whether to smile or look serious for her license photograph. Unfortunately, that comes down to looking like the Joker or looking like someone who's trying to see a fly on her nose.

As they're standing there, debating the topic, hard-up Holly and dashing Roger (William Bumiller), who is standing behind her, realize they'd met briefly at the lost and found; sparks fly and they make a date.

Meanwhile, as Ellen steps up to have her photo taken, the photographer (Matt Landers) says something that makes her angry—and *then* snaps the shot. Ellen is miffed, as the photo makes her look rabid.

Back at the apartment, Anita informs Ellen and Adam that she's learned through a mutual friend, Steve, that Roger is an attorney—who happens to bark "like Arsenio Hall during intercourse."

Upon hearing this, Ellen stalks around the room with disgust. "It's good that I know this," she says, "because now, if she marries him and spends the rest of her life with him, I'm going to have to think about this every time they come over for a barbecue."

What Ellen calls the "major inter-gender ordeal," Holly's date, is a success, so Ellen is free to concentrate on her own terrible problem: returning to the Department of Motor Vehicles and having a new photo taken. Dressed to kill, she steps in front of the camera and smiles—and smiles and smiles. This time the photographer is on the phone, ignoring Ellen as he talks his young son through a bowel movement. Ellen finally becomes impatient and starts to bitch; naturally, at that moment, he snaps the picture.

Later, at the apartment, Ellen tears both licenses up, telling Adam, "I'm into this for seventy bucks, I may as well go till I get it right."

Meanwhile, through friend Steve, Anita learns that Roger is planning to sleep with Holly and then dump her.

"Men," Ellen says to Adam, "men are scum."

The three musketeers decide to drive to Holly's

place and head them off, though Ellen takes the precaution of calling and leaving a message on the answering machine, revealing Roger's plans and adding that he "is a lying, sneaky, slimy, slug of a slug."

En route, Ellen is pulled over for speeding. Needless to say, the police officer also gives her a ticket for driving without a license.

The three friends arrive at Holly's too late to stop the couple from going to bed, though they're in time to hear the woofing.

"I think we're too late," Ellen says with a sigh as they huddle outside the window, listening to Roger.

Adam says hopefully, "Maybe they're just watching Arsenio."

When the couple emerge from the bedroom, the friends overhear Roger admit to Holly that although he intended to dump her after tonight, he's discovered that he's in love with her and wants to be with her always. Just then she sees the flashing message light on the answering machine: Ellen hurries to the door and rings the bell to keep her from listening to it. Then she informs Holly that they came to borrow . . . the answering machine.

She goes to get it, Holly tries to stop her, and as the two fight over it, the message comes on. As her recorded voice fills the room, Ellen observes sheepishly, "This certainly is awkward."

What ticks Holly off is that he told Steve, "that leering, butt-scratching blabbermouth," everything.

Holly throws Roger out, then confides to her friends that there was nothing to worry about: She had intended to dump *him* that night anyway.

"But," she adds, "I figured, I got him here, I might as well sleep with him first."

"Women!" Adam says indignantly. "Women are scum!"

16
A Hit and a Ms.

The worst part of having success is to try finding someone who is happy for you.

—Bette Midler

The "buzz" on the finished product was very good, and everyone at Touchstone was quite high on it. Best of all, ABC loved *These Friends of Mine* and gave the producers the go-ahead to shoot six shows, a half-season's worth, and to write half a dozen more. When word came to the Black/Marlens office, there were hugs and high-fives all around. Ellen was happy but reserved. There was a lot of work to do, fast—they needed to commission more scripts and come up with a shooting schedule— and the most important opinion had yet to be heard: the public's. From the start, Ellen insisted that it was the audience—not her, not the producers, and not the network—who would control the show.

"We're always thinking of our viewers," she told *Us* magazine. "Whatever they want to see, we'll give it to them. If they want to see Arye [Gross, who plays Adam] in a monkey suit, so it shall be. If they want to see Holly naked so we can compete with *NYPD Blue*—whatever."

That, of course, was Ellen's somewhat comedic view of things for the press. In truth, though she didn't realize it at the time, once the show took off there was going to be only one person calling the shots. Especially after she'd learned that the first episode wasn't going to air quite the way it had been shot.

There were trims here and there, most notably a reduction of the number of "woofs" guest star Bumiller barks during the sex scene. It's inconceivable that edits like these still go on in these cable-wired, post–*NYPD Blues* days, but they do; as *TV Guide* correctly observed, "Apparently, they [the censors] know just how many barks it takes to offend America."

Actually, Ellen herself wasn't too happy with the barking aspect of the show. "In my stand-up," she says, "I do an hour and a half or two of clean comedy. Because the show was created around me and because in essence I'm playing myself, I'm really sensitive to things like that.

"It's not that I'm offended by the guy in the pilot barking, but it certainly isn't something I would have written. It's just not me."

And the hint of future troubles began to rear its head because of just that aspect of the show. At the 1993 summer Television Critics Press Tour, when the networks' stars and shows are introduced to TV columnists and critics, Ellen was visibly uncomfortable being put in the position of having to defend the barker. At a press conference, she repeatedly tried to joke her way out of the questions, but the reporters wouldn't let her off the hook.

"They kept asking, 'Why were you clean for so long and now you're doing this?' I don't want people to think I'm suddenly doing something else or changing because I'm on TV. The thing is, I was totally out of the loop.

"I wish I were as powerful as Roseanne and knew everything that was going on and had a part of everything, but I'm certainly not that powerful."

After the episode was in the can, the theme music also underwent a change. The four friends strolling in the wide-open spaces, playing footsie in a kiddie pool and then sitting on a sofa to watch TV (still in some remote wilderness) was New Age enough without the *ohhh-oh, yeah, yeah* vocals on the soundtrack. Those were replaced with good old safe instrumentals.

Ellen was annoyed with some of the changes but not enough to make a stink. Yet.

Originally, *These Friends of Mine* was supposed to debut in the fall of 1993. However, sensing that they had a hit on their hands, ABC wanted to position it in the coveted post–*Home Improvement* slot to ensure that viewers would tune in. Unfortunately, they also wanted to put the new *Grace Under Fire* in that time slot, a half-hour sitcom starring another woman stand-up, Brett Butler, as a single mom who works at an oil refinery. Produced by the people who made *Roseanne*—and who wield considerable clout around the network—*Grace Under Fire* won out. It became the highest-rated new show of the season, and Ellen was forced to cool her heels for six months, until *Grace Under Fire* went on hiatus and her show could be slotted.

Ellen weathered the wait well. As "executive consultant" for her show (a rather euphemistic title meaning that she wasn't writing the stories or producing the show but still carried a lot of weight on both fronts), she huddled with the writers and producers to make sure that the scripts were as good as could be.

The debut of the show was finally scheduled for March of 1994.

Shortly before *These Friends of Mine* first aired, Ellen told reporters that she was confident the show would be a hit.

"I have grandmothers who come to my comedy shows, and I think they are going to watch my TV show," she joked with *Esquire* magazine. "Anyway," she added, "they've told me they will."

In a somewhat more serious vein, she told *Entertainment Weekly* magazine, "I don't know why, but whenever I've had this gut feeling, I've always been right." She added for good measure, "Now if this is

printed and I fail miserably, I'll be embarrassed."
(She would add that her gut only works where her
career is concerned: "I'm not like this in Las
Vegas," she says, where she loses a bundle playing
cards whenever she's booked at one of the hotels.)

Feeling even more confident as the debut drew
near, she went so far as to confess to *The New York
Times,* "I told my friends it would be the number-
three show." Why not number one? Ellen didn't
say, but she probably felt that it would have been
just a little presumptuous to suggest that she could
beat *Roseanne* and *Home Improvement.*

ABC decided to try something unusual with the
show, both to give it a one-two punch and to see
how it would perform in two different time slots.
After pulling *Grace Under Fire* temporarily to give
it a berth, they scheduled the first episodes to air on
two successive nights: March 29, where it would
follow *Roseanne* in the lineup, and March 30,
where it would air after *Home Improvement.*

And they promoted it extensively. For the week
before the debut, it was virtually impossible to turn
on an ABC show and not see a plug for Ellen.

Of course, that *really* put the pressure on: If she
bombed after all the hoopla, in those two plum
spots, the two most coveted time slots on television, she would be washed up on TV. Think *The
Chevy Chase Show,* move it from late night to the
more visible prime time, multiply it sixfold, and
you can begin to get the idea of what a failure
would have meant to her image.

Ellen was nervous but excited. Fortunately, they were in the midst of shooting the first batch of six episodes for the show, so she had the work to keep her busy. But it *was* difficult to concentrate. Ellen had always liked putting her talent on the line, and this was high-stakes poker indeed.

And there was more than just her reputation and ego on the line. In just the few weeks she'd been working on the lot, she'd grown to love the studio environment. Who wouldn't? It's Disneyland, it's a living museum of movie history, it's glamour, it's wealth and fame, it's a daily creative outlet. And it was different from *Open House* and *Laurie Hill,* where she had a tiny trailer for a dressing room and little contact with the movers and shakers.

More so than when she first started on *These Friends of Mine,* she wanted to keep it. And overnight, with just this roll of the dice, she could lose it all or it could be hers for years to come.

(John Ritter's advice to people in this situation is sound: "In terms of the pressure, you feel like you're swimming twenty thousand leagues under the sea naked. All you can do in this situation is approach it like you're going to have a good time.")

That Tuesday, March 29, was nervewracking. It seemed as though early evening would never come: six-thirty Pacific Time, nine-thirty Eastern, when the show would debut. She half-jokingly asked someone at the lot to explain to her again why they couldn't get the ratings at 10:01.

Wasn't all this stuff computerized? How come a computer could be so fast that if you made a phone call from your hotel room and then rushed to check out, the call would be right there on your bill—yet they couldn't do simple addition and tell her right away how many people had just watched her show?

They just couldn't, she was told. Network executives had to wait until morning, around eight o'clock Eastern, for the "overnights."

Okay, Ellen figured. At least if she couldn't sleep, she knew just where she'd be at five o'clock Pacific Time: on the phone to New York.

Though the wait was agony—and though she *was* able to get to sleep—the results were worth it.

Ellen didn't have to eat her words. Not exactly, anyway. *These Friends of Mine* was a smash on its debut night, landing at the top of the ratings, though only in the number-seven position.

She went to the lot full of questions. Was that good enough? Were the demographics close to what they'd wanted? Was the network happy? Would C-Span have scored in that time slot just because it came after *Roseanne?*

The second night erased all her fears as the show scored even higher ratings: It landed in the number-three position, to be exact.

Even more encouraging, however, is that research conducted by ABC showed that *These Friends of Mine* wasn't just a hit due to "sampling" —that is, viewers tuning in to see what the heavily promoted show was about. They sampled *and* they enjoyed what they saw enormously; a large number of viewers said they intended to watch the show again wherever it turned up.

Ellen had her hit.

17

Pressing Engagements

Sometimes I worry about being a success in a mediocre world.

—Lily Tomlin

Lily is right to worry.

More than any other outlet, TV encourages mediocrity. As *Mad* magazine once noted, "Why do you think they call it a medium?"

Lily and other incisive stand-ups are particularly frustrated because network TV seems to encourage stereotypes, especially among women. And the ones who break from that are typically presented as somewhat freakish on movies of the week.

"I think it's going to die hard, any kind of change," Lily laments. "There are a whole lot of people out there whose existence is built on certain kinds of values and behavior. The slightest challenge to it—at least, they interpret it as a challenge, rather than just a facet of existence—is something they can't tolerate. Which is pretty amazing, when you consider how many women are out there watching television!"

Ellen's comedy has never been as socially relevant as Lily's or as biting as that of stand-ups like Whoopi Goldberg and Marsha Warfield. But it *has* been personal, and it certainly hasn't been mediocre. It assumes that the audience has some level of sophistication, which is something that TV rarely does.

When she first agreed to do the show, Ellen had expected that she'd be able to retain a fair share of her personal, intelligent style of humor—despite the fact that she'd be playing to a prime-time television audience. And she wasn't the only one who saw how important that was.

Two months before *These Friends of Mine* debuted, columnist James Brady, who's almost always on the mark, wrote in *Parade* magazine that "Ellen is beautiful. She's smart. And—most important to her current success—she is very, very funny." He said that if *These Friends of Mine* "has halfway-decent scripts and lets Ellen do her stand-up thing, it ought to work."

The truth is, about thirty million people *did* like it—including her old friend Gladys Johnson. After watching the first two episodes, she said that not only did she love the show, but she was amazed at how much Ellen Morgan and Ellen DeGeneres are one and the same.

"She's totally herself, the way she looks, the way

she acts, and the way she dresses. That's totally Ellen."

That honesty, of course, is part of her appeal. Audiences sense honesty, whether it's Roseanne Arnold or Tim Allen: They know when a performer believes in the character she or he is playing.

The trouble was, as the weeks went on, Ellen began to feel less and less honest. She began to think that a lot of the "comedy" got lost in whatever "situation" she and her friends found themselves. And she began to have second thoughts about some of the scripts, especially as they went into rehearsal.

She didn't do anything about it, not at first. In those early weeks after the debut, what was most important to Ellen was to get out there and promote the show, to fortify her position in the top ten before she started worrying about fine-tuning or even overhauling the series.

She promoted the show with her characteristically zany public face.

"You'll laugh, you'll cry, you'll sneeze, you'll dance," she told one reporter. "Wait a minute. That's the side effects of taking too much cold medicine."

Well, it gets their attention, anyway.

Within four weeks, she says she was interviewed "easily two hundred or three hundred times. I can't believe there are that many people out there who still want to talk to me." Sometimes she'd be up at three-thirty in the morning to do six-thirty interviews in the east. Sometimes the interviews bordered on the inane—a condition she parodied in her *Us* self-interview when she asked the classic "bad interview" question: "If you were a tree, what kind would you be?" (Her answer: "A sticker bush." Reconsidering, she said, "Joshua. They live to be 150 years old, and no two are alike.")

Ever the good trooper, she even agreed to cohost, with Joey Lawrence, Jerry Van Dyke, and others, the dippy ABC special *Before They Were Stars,* which showed clips and photographs of superstars when they were just starting out.

Only once did Ellen complain about the grind, and with good reason.

Shortly after *These Friends of Mine* debuted, Ellen went to New York to appear on *The Late Show with David Letterman.* She was hot, she was in demand—and she was bounced.

While Ellen alternately cracked jokes and stewed in the green room at the former Ed Sullivan Theatre, just north of New York's Times Square, guest Jack Lemmon reminisced . . . and reminisced . . . and reminisced.

Staff members of the show helped to keep Ellen calm, especially when it became obvious that her spot wasn't going to be small, it wasn't going to be at all. When the late-afternoon taping wrapped, David hurried backstage, apologized profusely to Ellen—whom he has known for years—and literally begged her to stay in New York and come back the following night.

"Sorry," she said curtly. "I have a career waiting for me."

But Letterman and his staff didn't give up. They did what one press report called "some pampering —including a 'small shopping spree,'" and Ellen softened.

She came back the following night, and after introducing her, Letterman was effusive in his praise of Ellen and her show. Ellen soaked it in, after which Letterman began to rib her, Ellen parrying his thrusts with barbs of her own.

18

That Show
of Hers

*The TV show is more or less about me, or
someone like me.*

—Ellen DeGeneres

The sense of accomplishment Ellen felt was fleeting
as she became more and more concerned about the
show. For if, as Ellen and Gladys suggest, the
character was totally Ellen, the show wasn't.

Even though subsequent episodes featured Ellen
in almost every scene, allowing her to serve as a
Greek chorus as she was paired with one or more of
those friends of hers, the situations in which they
found themselves tended to range from the absurd
to the contrived and predictable.

Among the former was an embarrassingly inane
and unlikely episode in which Ellen and the gang
are blackmailed into helping young Maria (Sully
Diaz) smuggle her children out of Mexico under
the pretense of having gone south to buy some

artwork. Ellen ends up getting caught by a border guard (Patrick Mickler) and thrown in prison.

Another utterly improbable episode—written by co-executive producers Rosenthal and Warren Bell, who should have known better—had Ellen's "sweet and innocent" cousin Tracy (Joanna Daniels) paying a visit from Missouri. When biker-author Nester Biggs (Steven Gilborn) does a book signing, Tracy runs off with him, and Ellen, Holly, and Adam must go to the biker bar to bring her back. ("If that pig has hurt her," Ellen vows,"I'll . . . I'll . . . take his books off the new and noteworthy table!")

This episode wasn't Lucy; it was *Pee-wee's Big Adventure* without the benefit of Pee-wee. The best part of the show were the outtakes that ran under the closing credits: Gilborn misspeaking as he tried to do a reading from one of his books, and Ellen cracking up as a cheerful young woman (Jill Talley) invites Ellen and Tracy to the taping of an infomercial.

Among the better shows—albeit, one with way more sex than Ellen wanted—was the one in which Susan needs a date for a wedding. Ellen wants to help and first considers getting Susan a date with a strip-club operator, then with a transsexual, and finally with Adam, who proves to be a sexual dynamo but a bore and gets dumped. (Male-bashing is safe, after all. It's a crisis when someone uses Holly for sex but a joke when it happens to Adam.)

A high-school reunion episode was also sweet,

but it lacked the substance of a once-slim, now-heavy Delta Burke going back to *her* class reunion on *Designing Women*.

The stories weren't the only problems in the early shows. There were never enough moments when Ellen could do what she did best: the short, *honest,* stand-up "bits."

Despite everyone's best efforts, Ellen's stand-up asides usually ended up seemingly shoe-horned into the scripts—which, of course, they were. For example, she'd be sitting in a restaurant, signaling to the waiter to bring the check, and would suddenly ask, "What am I doing? What is this kind of gesture? Am I writing something, am I making a check mark?" It's supposed to be one of those "things that everyone does but never thinks about" moments, but it comes across as forced.

Or, unbeknownst to Ellen, after Susan and Adam have only just met and slept together, Ellen runs into Susan in the kitchen. Caught off-guard, Ellen fumbles through: "I've been *meaning* to have you over. This is like a slumber party except that, y'know, someone forgot my invitation. Not that I would've wanted to join ya. Two is company, three is sick. It is. Ménage-à-yuck, if you ask me." What should have been comedy springing from an awkward moment—something we've all experienced—became uninspired babble, and it stopped the show dead in its tracks.

Even worse, though, was this one: "People always think they look like celebrities," Ellen tells Adam in one episode, "but only the most beautiful ones.

Nobody ever says, 'I like old movies and walks on the beach, and by the way I'm a dead ringer for Don Rickles.'"

Don Rickles? The Wolfman or Cruella De Vil might've made the comment absurdly amusing. Besides, the truth is that most people *don't* think they look like celebrities. Where was the "DeGenerese" truth in that observation?

Or in this false and predictable progression: "In high school," she says, "when my hair was longer, people were always telling me that I looked exactly like Farrah Fawcett." Pause. "Not always but, y'know, now and again." Pause. "Once."

We knew that was coming. What Ellen would've done with that onstage—what would have been *funny*—would have been to learn who'd said it and why. (And what Mary Tyler Moore did with a line like that on *her* show was also much better. "I'm an experienced woman," she said. "I've been around. Well, all right, I might not have been around, but I've been . . . nearby." We knew *something* was coming, because Mary hadn't been around, but we didn't expect that. Watching Mary come up with just the right phrase was a hoot.)

Like Ellen's act, so many of the jokes on her show also relied on the classic comedy setup of "threes." That is, the comic uses two believable statements that allow the listener to become complacent, then follow it with a surprise statement, the "zinger." Unlike her act (like the club soda bit on the airplane, or the rack-of-lamb line), the threes here weren't funny.

For example, when Ellen has to break the news to Adam that Susan doesn't want to see him again, she tells him that Susan "couldn't stop talkin' about you all day long. Fabulous dancer, fabulous lover, never wants to see you again."

The problem was that the audience already knew that she didn't want to see him, so the zinger fell flat.

Or, following a visit to the beach with cousin Tracy, Ellen laments, "Spoil-sport scientists don't want you to have any fun anymore. Don't lay out in the sun, don't eat fatty foods, don't swim in raw sewage."

That's not only predictable (they've already discussed the contaminated water!), it isn't funny.

Not every scene and gag was weak, of course. One marvelous bit in the kid-smuggling episode had Ellen pitted against the guard on the Mexican border. When he asks for her papers, she rages, "Look, pal. We don't have any papers. We're citizens of the U.S. of A., and just because her two little children happen to have a darker shade of skin doesn't give you the right to question their nationality or harass my friends or treat us like we're some kind of second-class citizens. We're human beings, dammit, and we're just exercising our God-given right to life, liberty, and the pursuit of happiness."

The guard replies quietly, "That's all well and good, ma'am, but I'm talking about the artwork. I need to see your import-export papers."

Cut to Ellen, who does the egg-on-the-face bit very well.

Even better was the followup phone call to her mother. After some everyday kind of chitchat, Ellen says, "One more thing real quick. I'm in a Mexican prison and I need you to send fifteen hundred dollars to post bail. Mom . . . Mom . . . don't 'Oh, Ellen,' me. . . ." For everyone who's ever had to call home for help in a bad situation, it was one of the show's few moments of truth.

Another fun exchange occurred between Susan and Ellen at the bookshop. After Ellen has set up a display of books about fun things to do on the weekend, Susan comes in and complains, "What is this obsession with having fun on the weekend? Why can't it be enough to just sit at home and wonder whatever happened to your life?"

Ellen looks at her and replies, "I'll see if we have a book on that!"

Ellen wasn't happy, but the producers told her not to worry. The show was working with viewers and she'd be crazy to mess with something that was so successful.

She tried to go with the flow, but the drag was becoming more pronounced. She was already thinking of what life would be like after *These Friends of Mine*. Roseanne Arnold had fought for the integrity of *her* show, won, and could return to stand-up if she wanted, unbowed. Or she could retire with the fortune she'd made from creating a series that was true to her and was admired by the viewing public—in spite of network cold feet over its more controversial episodes.

Would Ellen be able to do the same? Especially if she weren't funny, or ended up—as was more and more the case—as not just a Greek chorus but a "straight woman" for the antics of Adam and Holly?

Settling for something that wasn't quite right gnawed at her more and more. So what if it was popular? *It wasn't right.*

The critics only added to Ellen's distress, though they didn't pick up on the same things that were bothering her. Perhaps, being television critics, they were accustomed to the banal.

Rather, it seemed as though almost every critic who wrote about the show felt that it was a reverse clone of *Seinfeld:* Instead of three young, funny, oddball guys and a lady doing the relationship-career shuffle in New York, it was three young, funny, oddball ladies and a guy doing the relationship-career shuffle in Los Angeles.

TV Guide accurately summed up the differences between the shows by noting that the characters lack "the easy, amplified idiosyncrasies" of the *Seinfeld* crew, that Ellen and her friends are "quieter, saner—truer," and that Ellen herself is "incredibly engaging" instead of "amusingly whiny" like Seinfeld. But that didn't stop the comparisons from dominating the press.

Disturbing as this was, none of it was exactly new to Ellen.

"I've always been compared to Jerry," the exasperated comedian told *The New York Times.* Yet, she said, "if you saw my act, we're not very much alike at all. I like the observational stuff. There's a brilliance to finding a simple thing. I love that stuff, but it's like the lowest common denominator. I like taking you on the whole ride."

The observational material, she says, is "basically his whole thing, and that's a very small part of mine." She told *USA Today*, "Had I made it before him, they'd probably be calling him the male Ellen DeGeneres."

(Asked what he thinks of Ellen and her show, Jerry says sincerely, "They're both terrific. I'm glad she's not on opposite me.")

Since the comedians were always being compared, Ellen says it was no surprise to her that the shows would be compared.

At first, Ellen dismissed the comparisons with humor.

"Well," she told one reporter, "our kitchen is on the other side of the set." She added that, yes indeed, the shows are so similar that "they're even trying to get me to dress more like him." (Though said in jest, Ellen's character *does* favor jeans and a sweater or blazer.)

Ironically, after the critics got tired of comparing it to *Seinfeld*—or realized that the comparison wasn't valid—they took a different tack. As Ellen told one reporter, *"Now* people are comparing it to *The Mary Tyler Moore Show*. Pretty soon it'll be *Flipper."*

In a very short time, comparisons with *any* show began to get on Ellen's nerves. She didn't understand why critics had to pigeonhole her or anyone.

Hollywood entertainment attorney Steve Burkow was right on the money when he pointed out that it had nothing to do with Ellen, really. Rather, the post–*Seinfeld* airwaves were "like the post–*Die Hard* action movies. You had *Under Siege,* which was described as '*Die Hard* on a boat,' *Passenger 57,* which was called '*Die Hard* on a plane,' and *Speed,* which was '*Die Hard* on a bus.'

"Maybe," he said, "Ellen should be thankful for the *Seinfeld* comparisons. Otherwise the critics might've described her show as '*Die Hard* in a bookstore.'"

But Ellen wasn't thankful. To the contrary. Because of the frustrating perception of the show, and scripts that weren't quite what they should have been, she grew increasingly annoyed as each week passed.

19

Feeling
DeGeneres

*I don't want any yes-men around me. I want
everybody to tell me the truth even if it costs
them their jobs.*

—Samuel Goldwyn

John Ritter has some sound advice for people who
are unhappy doing television—or doing anything
else, for that matter. "If people would just approach their work about fifteen days throughout the
year," he says, "and remember the joy you felt
when you started out, and why you wanted to do
this work in the first place, things would be much
easier for them and for those around them.

"The problem is, too many people *don't* want to
do what they're doing. They want to do what
someone else is doing. Or they want someone to do
what they're supposed to be doing *for* them. I've
looked forward to being with colleagues that I can

141

goof around with or learn something from—but once there's this tension of 'Listen, kid, you're working for me,' or 'Hey, buddy, that was my line,' then you can't really have fun."

After six weeks of going with the flow, of seeing if she felt more comfortable with the show, its relatively soft comedy, and its relatively hard sex, Ellen wasn't having a lot of luck or very much fun.

She was feeling worse than ever about the quality of the material and the focus of the scripts, and that frustration drove her to suggest (or insist, depending upon who one asks at the set) that the stories focus more on her and less on the ensemble, and that she spend more time "executive consulting" during the writing process.

Concern with the quality and subject matter was certainly a large part of Ellen's motivation. But was she also driven by the desire to make herself the unequivocal center of attention? Was she desperate to keep Ellen Morgan, the linchpin of the show, from being overshadowed by frankly more quirky and interesting characters?

Any time a TV star becomes successful, he or she tends to take greater control of the vehicle that made them successful, either in name or in fact. Sometimes the actor has the show's best interests at heart: They want to make sure that writers, directors, or network executives—some of them newly hired—don't come in and muck with what makes the formula work.

By and large, that's what happened on *Roseanne*.

And it was also the case with *Ellen*'s prime-time stablemate, *Grace Under Fire*.

As Brett Butler, star of the latter show explained it (and she might just as well have been talking for Ellen), the scripts were lame and "people weren't agreeing with me at the script meetings. I stood up and said, 'You should use me, you should let me help. I can't sing or dance, but I am really good at *this.*' So I went in at night and on weekends to work with the writers." When one of them protested that she wasn't a writer, Brett says, "I resisted the impulse to say, 'C'mere, I've read more books than you even know the names of.'"

Sometimes, though, it's just the star's swelled head: That was what helped to eclipse *Moonlighting,* to name just one of many shows.

Sometimes the takeover is amicable; sometimes it's hostile and litigious. And once in a rare while the star loses: In 1991, when Delta Burke reportedly tried to wrest *Designing Women* from creators Linda Bloodworth-Thomason and Harry Thomason, CBS backed the Thomasons.

To many people who worked at the production offices, at the studio, and at the network, the power struggle with producers Black and Marlens was more a result of Ellen's ego than a desire for quality control. And some measure of ego cannot be ruled out, though it appears to have been a small part of the forces at work.

Ellen did, quite naturally, feel that this was her show. Meanwhile, the other actors had been hired with the promise that this was going to be an ensemble series. Otherwise, *These Friends of Mine* were not notches that either Ayre Gross or Holly Fulger needed on their belts. They'd already *done* the supporting-role bit.

The seeds of discontent were planted early.

When Ellen was asked to do virtually all of the publicity for the show, Fulger and Gross were hurt but they kept their disappointment pretty much to themselves. Ellen *was* funny and made for good copy, so they let it slide.

But after a few weeks, the read-throughs started to take on a confrontational atmosphere. One of the regular attendees says that it was common for Ellen to zero in on all the good lines Holly was getting, wondering why they weren't hers. Also, she failed to understand why the writers were promoting her as the cute, funny one.

"Isn't that supposed to be *my* role?" she once asked.

When the star of a hit TV show asks that question, the only possible response is "Yes."

One of the production-company employees gripes, "Roseanne Arnold was smart enough to surround herself with good people, like John Goodman and Laurie Metcalf, and let them have as many jokes and good scenes as they could. Roseanne understood that their success would make her look good, especially in the early days when she was learning how to be a good sitcom actor.

"Ellen isn't like that."

What, then, *is* she like? Is she a control freak driven solely by ego?

"Not at all," says a representative of ABC, who would be expected to put a good face on things. "Her appeal is central to the success of the show, so why shouldn't we focus more on her? Besides, the situation isn't comparable to *Roseanne.* That's a show about a family. Everyone is expected to share the spotlight and the laughs. This is a show about Ellen."

Another view, voiced by an actor who has appeared on the show, is that, unlike Holly and Ayre, who have done dramatic work, Ellen hasn't. "She isn't secure enough as an actress," says the actor, "to stand there and *not* get laughs. She doesn't feel comfortable doing 'serious,' so of course she wants the jokes for herself."

Again, a spokesperson for Ellen says that that's absurd, and one is inclined to agree: At times, she's done some very dramatic and moving material in her act.

There were other developments, somewhat more dramatic, throughout May and June of 1994.

First, before filming resumed late in the summer, Ellen asked (some say *demanded*) that shooting be moved from the Sony lot over to the Disney Studios in the San Fernando Valley. That put it much closer to Ellen's home, and, the roads still clogged with postearthquake traffic, not having to use the surviving freeways made Disney much easier to get to. (Though not everything was better on Dopey Drive: The soundstage to which they moved her didn't have a dressing room. Unlike at Sony, Ellen had to retire to a mobile home next to the soundstage whenever she wasn't needed.)

Second, the cast got their walking papers—sort of. Now, cast changes are not new in TV. Meg Foster, the actress who'd been originally slated to costar on *Cagney and Lacey,* was unceremoniously canned in favor of now-rich Sharon Gless; the late Jeffrey Hunter had William Shatner's part in the original *Star Trek* pilot, which failed to sell; Mike Henry and Lyle Waggoner were both up for the role of TV's Batman, only to be passed over in favor of Adam West. Choices like these hurt, but that's show biz. Usually, however, that happens *before* a show airs. This was different.

The character of Anita was eliminated, and both Holly and Adam were cut way back. That was bad news for Holly Fulger and Arye Gross: Not only would they have less to do, but they would get less money. They would only be paid for episodes in which they appeared, and they were tentatively set to act in just six of the thirteen shows ordered for the first half of the season. It is reported that at least one of them asked to be released from their contract but was turned down; if it were demonstrated, after a few shows had been shot, that Ellen couldn't carry the series more or less on her own, the "friends" could always be brought back. But not if they had already taken parts on a different sitcom or were off shooting a movie.

Though one of the actors suggested Ellen may

have been behind the firings—motivated by jealousy at who was getting more laughs—a spokesperson for Ellen says that Touchstone Television, not Ellen, ordered the cutbacks for budgetary reasons.

"Many TV shows are cutting back," he said. "This season [1994–1995] a number of half-hour network sitcoms had to cut roughly one-fifth of their budgets, about $200,000 a week, or face cancellation. That happened to *Evening Shade. These Friends of Mine* is no exception.

"You can't very well drop Ellen from her own show, and production costs are standard. So where are the cuts going to come from? It *has* to be from the cast."

That bugged Holly and Arye to no end, as it had to have bothered Maggie Wheeler. They had all suffered through the stages of "Will I get the part?" then "Will the pilot sell?" and finally "Will we be a hit?" Now they were on a show that had turned out to be a smash, on which a supporting player could make twenty or thirty thousand dollars a week in addition to millions more in residuals. Instead of that, however, they were going to be earning relative peanuts. This just weeks after Holly had celebrated by going out and buying herself a new home.

"Ellen could've taken a cut," said a spokesperson for one of them. "I think all of the actors would have agreed to salary cuts to make up the deficit. They were loyal to the show. And they were also loyal to each other."

(The tense situation of being potential part-time

players came to an end in mid-June, when Fulger and Gross were officially released from their contracts.)

Third, the original team at the Black Marlens Company relinquished hands-on control over the show and were replaced by Ellen's hand-picked people. That move was widely rumored to have been made to keep the exproducers from crossing swords with Ellen; as one employee said, "They've moved from out of the background to out of the building. We've been joking that we can start planning a spinoff, *These Ex-Friends of Mine.*"

However, the producers deny any friction with Ellen and point out that they had relinquished hands-on control over *The Wonder Years* after a single season as well. They say that they enjoy concentrating on new projects once hit shows have already been launched.

Finally, Ellen wanted the name of the show changed from *These Friends of Mine* to *Ellen.* This was intended to underscore who the show was going to be about—or who was the star, if you ask some of Ellen's co-workers. This was one of the names the producers had originally considered; and an ABC representative said, "It fits in with popular shows like *Roseanne* and *Dave's World* which use names in the title"; nevertheless, the timing of the change was terrible. It only added logs to the fire that was already raging over Ellen's ego being out of control.

What does Ellen say in her own defense?

Not much.

For one thing, she doesn't pay much attention to criticism about ego and vanity.

"If you work in an office," she says, "it's all based on performance. You have to do your job well and be nice to your co-workers and boss. But with this profession, you want to perform well enough to please millions of people, which is, of course, impossible." The only thing you can do, she believes, is "be true to yourself and hope there are people who like what you do."

Ellen shrugged off rumors of a feud with the producers without actually addressing whether or not one had broken out. She told *Entertainment Weekly,* "I've heard all kinds of rumors about that, but we're all still good friends."

As for Black and Marlens, while they acknowledge that they quit after the first six shows, they did so, they say, for "personal" reasons.

The bottom line is that it's Ellen's reputation that's on the line, and a show as marginally funny as hers was becoming could destroy that reputation —even if people tune in because they're amused by what she can do with even a dull line. No one knows what's funny for Ellen the comedian better than Ellen, and she has every right to make sure that people who share her soundstage share her vision.

The trade press, periodicals like *The Hollywood Reporter* and *Variety,* reported all of these events matter-of-factly.

However, as soon as Ellen became a household name, she discovered that not every journalist was going to treat her with kid gloves. In fact, some of them—particularly those who worked for the tabloids—were about to make the pernicious critics seem like her biggest fans.

20

Full-Court Press

The public have an insatiable curiosity to know everything. Except what is worth knowing.

—Oscar Wilde

"I miss stand-up terribly," says Tim Allen with a sigh.

He says he doesn't just miss it because he loves going one-on-one with an audience. He misses it because when he was less famous, when he wasn't "Mr. Big, Big Hollywood TV Star," he didn't have to worry about the tabloid press constantly checking up on what he was doing.

"Life was much easier then. I knew that that rustling in the bushes was a cat, not a photographer trying to take my picture when I go to the mailbox. Like that's newsworthy. *Peace in the Middle East . . . and comedian gets swimsuit issue in mail.*"

Not that all the stories were quite so tame. As soon as Allen became famous, every tabloid newspaper and TV show was reporting about how, when he was a student at Western Michigan University in

Kalamazoo, Allen started dealing small amounts of drugs, which became larger amounts of drugs by the time he graduated in 1976. Two years later he was busted in the middle of a $43,000 deal at the Kalamazoo airport, and Allen was sentenced to twenty-eight months in prison.

Allen didn't think that was newsworthy either, but at least it was in the past and he'd paid his debt to society. The public fascination with his present-day private life mystifies him.

Indeed, very few celebrities understand the attention and are able to put it in perspective.

Delta Burke once complained that this is the only business where someone's garbage can be turned into news or a collectible.

Singer and actress Whitney Houston is more colorful in expressing her hostility. Sitting in her luxurious, very private suite at the Bel Air in Beverly Hills, Houston recently complained, "It goes with the territory, so they say. Well, fuck the territory. That's what *I* say. It's like a magazine soap opera. We're living soap operas to them. And if you try to sue them, it's another pain in the ass.

"And you think they're gonna stop writing or saying scandalous things if we go to court? I don't. If I could wipe them off the face of the earth, that would not only make my life a lot more peaceful, but a lot of other peoples' lives as well."

At the opposite end of the spectrum, Charlton Heston points out, "You can't reasonably expect to have the perks and the power of celebrity without the attention. And yes, you have to face cameras and questions whenever you go to a restaurant, and that may be unpleasant for some people. But it's also true that you never have to wait for a table at that restaurant, and your needs are looked after."

Most celebrities feel the same as Whitney. They believe that the press is responsible for the tension in their lives. The bulk of them also believe that they owe the public nothing more than their performance. If the press would only stay away, everything would be fine.

(However, many of these self-same stars dutifully keep abreast of what's in the supermarket tabloids. It's *amazing* who subscribes to and studies them. When they arrive by mail, usually on Tuesday mornings, the papers are required reading on many soundstages. It's also surprising how many crew members "rat" on abusive stars, and how many jealous celebrities provide information about rivals, noisy star neighbors, ex-lovers, etcetera.)

The stars and their handlers also work very hard to propagate the idea that much of what the tabloids print isn't true.

They're wrong, however, and they know it.

The three major tabloids—*The National Enquirer, The Star,* and *Globe*—have teams of tough, thorough, seasoned reporters and editors, and equally hard-nosed attorneys, who demand verification, corroboration, and very specific data from sources. While it's true that they get burned on occasion, this doesn't happen nearly as often as celebrity puffery would suggest. Many stars go through the heavily publicized motions of suing the tabloids, only to drop the case quietly after a few weeks.

The reason, of course, is that the majority of the stories are true.

The fact is that stars' lives *are* soap operas, a form of entertainment, and the fans who make these people rich and famous want to know more. Some fans are curious about how the stars look without makeup, without the careful lighting, without the expensive clothes. Others want to be reassured that the hero or heroine, comedian or dramatic star, is just as poised or intelligent or as wonderful or glamorous in real life.

Most aren't, which explains why so many of them shun publicity. Ellen herself says, "People see you play a character or see you on a talk show for about a five-minute interview, and they project some personality or image onto you from what they see. And it's probably not who you are, whether it be good or bad."

Still other tabloid consumers want just the opposite. They want to see how flawed the stars are in order to feel better about themselves. A star may have fame and wealth and clout, but that doesn't make them immune to failed relationships, serious weight problems, drug-dealing in their past—or what many people would consider to be out-of-the-ordinary sexual behavior.

Enter Ellen.

When she was selected Best Female Comedy Club Stand-up at the televised American Comedy

Awards in 1991, reporters didn't feel the need to go through her trash or examine her lifestyle. Who she dated, where she ate, and what she wore wasn't news.

But it was about to be.

A little over a year after Tim Allen made his remarks, when Ellen first taxied onto the runway for her takeoff into megacelebrity, she wasn't quite as jaded as her fellow stand-up. She understood how the synergy worked between fame and fandom.

She agreed with Tim Allen, in that she didn't think that someone like her, a stand-up on a TV series, deserves all the attention.

On the scale of people who should be written about, "I'd put schoolteachers way above me," she said, "or nurses."

However, she understood that being a public figure, especially an entertainer, was like living in a fish bowl. And "The more famous you get, the more people tap on the bowl, but they're the same people who feed you. I guess I feel an affinity with fish, and yet I had sushi for dinner last night. I'm a cannibal. . . . Oh my God!"

(She did go out of her way to say, though, that in case a reporter or fan tries to get to her, she now keeps a book beside her bed, *How to Kill an Intruder in Your Home.* She admits, however, "I haven't read it yet, so I'll just throw it. It's heavy.")

Ellen's tolerance and glib patter vanished quickly after she became one of the superfamous and felt the watchful eyes of the tabloid press constantly upon her. Worse, the tabloid press environment in which Ellen found herself was considerably more adversarial than it was when Tim Allen first faced it. There are more outlets than ever, each of them trying to beat out the others with information. And not just the tabloids, either. Mainstream publications from *The New York Post* to *People* have increased the number of reporters and stringers who are keeping "tabs" on celebrities 'round the clock, and TV shows like *Hard Copy* and *A Current Affair* are throwing larger amounts of money at friends or relatives or former lovers of the rich and famous for tell-alls.

The first time Ellen crossed swords with the media hounds, it was the mainstream press that got her, misrepresenting something she'd said while promoting the show. A magazine quoted her as saying that she didn't like being considered a comedian because "it's kind of like saying you're a clown."

Her remark seemed to be putting down clowns when, in fact, she'd meant nothing of the kind. What she was saying was that as soon as you wear a label, it limits you. She certainly didn't mean to imply that one was better than the other, but that was how it came out.

"Most of the time I do interviews, I read them and just shake my head," she complained in *Us* magazine. "It's so misconstrued, so out of context. I'm sitting there, thinking, 'This isn't what I said at all. I've never wanted to braid La Toya Jackson's hair.'"

But Ellen was smart enough to recognize that the potential for misrepresentation was greater if she *didn't* do interviews, or if a reporter got a story from someone else and she didn't make herself available to comment on it.

Suppose, she said, that "today some salesperson may give me an attitude, and I'll be a bitch, then she'll tell all her friends I'm a bitch and probably that I look better on TV, and then those friends will tell their friends and so on. Next thing you know, three thousand people think I'm a bitch, and by that time the story will be so blown out of proportion, it's now I've slapped a saleswoman who was pregnant, and that I'm fat and an alcoholic.

"But if I go home and tell a friend this salesperson is rude, I doubt they'll call anyone and say, 'Hey, there's a woman who works in the shoe department at the Broadway who is mean.'"

The problem is that Ellen, like so many other stars, will cooperate with the mainstream press but not with the tabloids. She'll go on *Entertainment Tonight* or host E!'s *Talk Soup*, appear with Kathy Lee and Regis or David Letterman or Jay Leno, or talk to *Mademoiselle* or *The New York Times* or *Esquire*. But she won't talk to the supermarket tabloids. Like many stars, she seems to fear that giving an interview suggests tacit approval of the *kinds* of stories they do. As a result, her relationship with the tabloids rapidly went from innocuous to deeply personal.

21
Keeping Tabs

It's not true I had nothing on. I had the radio on.

—Marilyn Monroe

Ellen once remarked, "People always ask me, 'Is your life as a performer that much different than ours? The little people. The nobodies. The scum.'"

When her show debuted, not many people knew —and Ellen liked it that way. But the status wouldn't remain quo for very long.

While promoting her show in March of 1994, Ellen told *USA Today* that her greatest fear about stardom was not the loss of privacy but that someone would dig up her high-school senior photograph.

"The picture is so bad," she told the newspaper. "It's scary."

She was joking, of course, but going on record with a statement like that is tantamount to waving the proverbial red flag in front of a bull. Within two weeks, *The National Enquirer* had found and published the 1976 photograph.

As it happens, the portrait is no more or less unflattering than any photo of any teenager with a seriously outdated hairdo and ingenuous smile. As Ellen's best friend from high school, Julie Battenfield, told the tabloid, "In the picture, Ellen's hair flipped out at the side. She was such a joker, everyone thought she'd done something to *make* the picture look funny. But she hadn't."

Ellen recognized the publication of the photo in *The National Enquirer* as a salvo fired across her bow. She understood that she was now fair game for the tabloids and that everything she said or did was going to be watched. For example, when she was photographed at an industry function beside towering Brett Butler, the comedians were dubbed the winners of "the Mutt and Jeff fashion award."

But Ellen was fatalistic enough to believe that it came with the fish bowl, that there was nothing she could do to prevent it, and that readers wouldn't believe everything they read.

As soon as Ellen's show debuted and was a smash, there was more to deal with than just the digging up of a yearbook photo. In June of 1994, a reporter for *The Star* wrote an accurate, well-researched article on the fate of the show's costars, claiming that Ellen is "power hungry now that her show's skyrocketed her to stardom." The piece talked about how scripts written around Gross and Fulger "were tossed," and how Ellen regarded the show as "an extension of her stand-up routine—which she did alone, so that's what she wants for next season."

Globe also ran an article on how the other actors were being cut back and "may appear in every third episode or so."

That same month, May, things got worse for Ellen as the *The National Enquirer* ran an article—bold even by their standards—the headline of which screamed:

> *These Friends of Mine* star told to watch those friends of hers. *TV's newest funny girl warned: Stay out of gay bars!* Producers fear her lifestyle will turn off viewers.

The article was accompanied by a photo of a smiling Ellen with her cheek pressed to the head of the "openly gay singer Melissa Etheridge" (who wrote the theme music for Ellen's show). The two of them were identified in the caption as "close pals," a tabloid euphemism that, as a rule, suggests that the people are more than that.

In the context of the article, the meaning was clear—especially since it included quotes from a friend who had "seen Ellen and Melissa sitting close, holding hands and talking about how they met at one of Melissa's concerts about three years ago."

The National Enquirer piece also featured another high-school photo of Ellen, looking extremely masculine in her tennis togs.

The article went on to explain how Ellen's friends "haven't seen her date a guy since a football

star [Ben Heath] broke her heart in high school"
back in Atlanta.

The reader could interpret *that* to mean that
Ellen has carried a torch for Heath ever since, like
Scarlett O'Hara for the dashing Ashley Wilkes—or
that the ill-fated romance turned her off to men
altogether. For unlike Scarlett, Ellen was not reported to have gone from one man to another.

Quite the opposite.

The article implied that she hung out with wom-
en, claiming that "most of Ellen's friendships with
lesbians have been [quite] public, especially when
she lived in New Orleans." Crystal Neidhart, a gay
woman who lives in New Orleans, told *The National Enquirer* reporters David Wright and Joe
Mullins that she saw Ellen at a French Quarter
lesbian bar with a beautiful young woman in 1982.

"Ellen always had her arm around the woman's
waist or shoulder," said Crystal. "I saw them slow
dance very close."

Crystal wasn't the only who had stories like that
to tell. At the time, rumors about Ellen's sexuality
became so pronounced that local deejay John Walton asked his listeners, "Has anybody ever known
this woman to be associated with a man in a
romantic way?" Walton told the *The National
Enquirer,* "Everyone said, 'No!' "

The article went on to report how these days, her
circle of friends is comprised of "a group of high-
profile Hollywood lesbians." It said that Ellen has
"been seen frequently at gay clubs and events," and

that among the numerous places she reportedly frequents are West Hollywood's lesbian dance club the Girl Bar, the Palms, and the She Club, where she can be found "talking quietly with dates over candlelit dinners."

Maybe Ellen believes, as Gloria Steinem once put it, that "a woman without a man is like a fish without a bicycle." But if Ellen feels that way she didn't deign to say so.

Does she have something to hide, or does she just feel that it's nobody's business? And are her producers, especially the executives at highly image-conscious Disney, really concerned?

When Ellen interviewed herself (!) for *Us* magazine and asked, "Do you have a boyfriend?" her response was "That's personal. I don't talk about my private life." She said that if she told a reporter that she *did* have a boyfriend, she'd have to reveal his name, his profession, and talk about whether they are happy. She didn't want that kind scrutiny. And if she said she *didn't* have a boyfriend, people would want to know why not and what's wrong with her.

Thus, she concluded, "My private life is just an area I choose to keep private. Hence the name *private life.*"

So at first she refused to comment about the report in *The National Enquirer.* However, her press representative at the time, Lori Jonas, did have something to say: She adamantly insisted that the story was untrue and denied that Ellen goes to "girl-only bars." She also said that, contrary to what was reported in *The National Enquirer,* the producers of *These Friends of Mine* didn't ask her to change or tone down her lifestyle.

Associates of the producers agree that Black and Marlens had "asked" for no such thing. All they'll admit is that there was "some talk" with Ellen about how best to respond to the article. Some advisers wanted to ignore it, others wanted to slam it hard, and still others wanted to counter with interviews in other magazines and newspapers. One staff worker rather lamely declared to a reporter that people shouldn't believe everything they read. After all, Ellen talks about a boyfriend in her act, and she'd told David Letterman on TV that "I really do want to have a baby." Which means nothing, of course. Besides, if readers can't believe a tabloid, why should they believe someone about a star when their paycheck depends upon that star?

An ABC representative was somewhat more forthcoming, on condition her name not be used: "Ellen is very comfortable with who she is, and she has never made a secret about her lifestyle. It would be sad if she had to change to appease anyone else.

"I think Ellen's personal life is her personal business. Case closed."

Ah, but it wasn't.

While it's true we can't always believe what we read, it's also true that we can't always believe what people tell us. Especially people who are on Ellen's payroll or who stand to lose millions of dollars. And for better or worse, right or wrong, enquiring minds want to know more—or at least the truth.

And what is the truth? It's everything *The National Enquirer* reported, and more. And while dismissing the reports in public, Ellen has scrambled to adjust in her private life.

One woman who is very close to Ellen says, "Ellen is the Diva right now among the upper echelon of gay women in L.A. Before she became a TV star, Ellen thought nothing of going out to lesbian bars and hanging with her friends there.

"The gay community in West Hollywood is very casual and laid back—it's no big deal. People are used to seeing famous faces at local gay clubs, and most gays are very protective of gay celebrities.

"Up until last year, it wasn't unusual to see Ellen at gay women's places like the Palms or the dance club Girl Bar or eating at places like Little Frieda's and the Abbey, which also cater to a gay clientele."

Now, however, in the wake of the TV show's success and the tabloid story, the woman says that "Ellen has started going underground, just a little bit. She's not as familiar a face in the gay bars anymore. Instead, now she's a part of the 'private house' scene."

Not surprisingly, says the woman, this can be a rewarding world for a star of Ellen's stature.

"As Ellen's star rose, so did the number of invitations to join this elite social group. Now Ellen is the queen bee. When she walks in—never alone, always accompanied by someone—every eye in the place turns her way. It's like Princess Di walked in."

Another friend reports that Ellen is "vaguely

uncomfortable with how cliquish this group is," but it's the only way she can go out and still be relatively safe from photographers. Besides, says the friend, for Ellen "to pretend to have a boyfriend or feel the need to create a life for public consumption that doesn't really exist is very stressful.

"Leading a double life wears you down, as many women in this 'crushed velvet' group can attest. Ellen seems torn between just saying 'the hell with it' and being who she is without trying to hide or make excuses . . . or staying in the closet so Middle America will love her unconditionally."

For now, says another friend, Ellen "has developed an entourage mentality, where she comes and goes surrounded by a gaggle of people in the hopes they'll keep the big bad world away. It's not that she's rude: If you go over and talk to her, she's pleasant.

"It's more a kind of shyness, like the neighborhood kids who stand off to the side because they're too shy to say they want to play."

After several weeks of questions from reporters, and discovering that her private is not as private as she might like, Ellen tried taking a slightly harder stand. On talk shows, she called the story sensationalistic and untrue. But that didn't stop the talk—first impressions are the ones that stick in the public mind—or stop reporters from talking to women who say they've seen her at these places.

While Ellen's handlers maintained their public denials, privately they were inclined to do what other stars have found successful through the years: They told the tabloid that Ellen might cooperate on innocuous stories like "At Home with . . . ," "My Favorite Holiday Recipes," "My Most Embarrassing Moment," and pieces of that type in exchange for the tabloid staying away from anything rougher. It wasn't that they had anything to hide, they said; they just didn't want Ellen's friends or family being harassed.

As it happens, tabloid readers like those "inside" reports as much as they do the more daring "keyhole" stories, and *The National Enquirer* was amenable to a deal. Unfortunately, the agreement became unraveled when the tabloid refused to tell Ellen's people the names of the sources who were helping them get information about the star's private life. Later, however, one of Ellen's representatives went back to the tabloid to try and revive the deal.

Whether Ellen eventually finalizes the arrangement or not, the problem isn't going to go away. Even if she puts out fires at *The National Enquirer* (which sells an average of 3.5 million copies a week, with a readership of some fifteen million), she'll still have to worry about the rival and highly competitive *The Star* and *Globe,* the number-two and -three circulation tabloids, respectively. And then, of course, there are the old friends, lovers, and family members who may want to write books about their life with Ellen.

* * *

Shortly before she became the new toast of prime time, Ellen braced herself for the attention and hard knocks she was sure to get. She said, "Anyone who complains should get out of the business."

True enough. And though she's disagreed with the coverage, she hasn't complained. Perhaps she should heed something Mary Tyler Moore said in the late 1970s when the collapse of her marriage, the suicide of her son, and other troubles made her the tabloids' pinup girl: "If you keep your feet on the ground, there's no way they can knock you on your butt."

Then again, maybe there's no point trying to fight it. A portion of the public will invariably get things wrong.

Sometime stand-up comic Mel Nehaus reports that a few days after the debut of *These Friends of Mine,* a TV fan went to Jerry Ohlinger's Movie Memorabilia Store in Manhattan to acquire photos of the new prime-time sensation.

He asked the young woman behind the counter for photos of the actress who stars in *These Friends of Mine.*

"What's her name?" asked the clerk.

The customer replied, "Ellen DeGenerate."

22
How I Spent My Summer Vacation

A celebrity is a person who works hard all his life to become well known, then wears dark glasses to avoid being recognized.

—Fred Allen

Even with her show off the air, Ellen managed to use it to amuse, thanks to her clever trade advertisements, in publications like *The Hollywood Reporter,* promoting her for an Emmy Award. One ad had her photo with the headline, "Mom, please don't cut this out and stick it on the fridge," while another read, "Well, here's Ellen. Just hanging out in the trades . . . No real reason . . . Phew, is it hot out there or what? . . . Almost summer . . . summer camp . . . mosquito bites . . . Calamine lotion . . . scabs . . . How about those Knicks?"

Though she may not get the Emmy for best actress in a comedy (rookies are not usually favored), the campaign deserves a Clio.

These Friends of Mine, now called *Ellen*, returned to the ABC weekly lineup in the fall. The network slotted it in the nine-thirty spot following *Roseanne* and right before *NYPD Blue*.

"Now I can go nude," Ellen crowed when she got the time period formerly occupied by *Coach*. It should have easy going, opposite *The CBS Tuesday Movie*, *The Fox Tuesday Movie*, and the struggling *Larroquette*.

ABC gave *Ellen* the choice place in the lineup because it views the show as having long legs, the heir apparent and an anchor for future hits, while the other shows are probably in or near their last seasons. Though *Ellen* may still be too new to stand on its own, after a few months of regular weekly broadcasts behind *Roseanne*, it will build a large and devoted audience of its own and can be moved anywhere.

And despite ongoing reports of egotism or perfectionism, depending on who you're talking to, Ellen vigorously defends the changes she has made.

Having seen other stars come and go, she says with some justification, "I'm not kidding myself—this is a weird business. Everyone wants to be your friend as long as you're successful and making them money." After that, it's on to the next flavor of the month.

But Ellen won't have to worry about being cast out for a while. If the pattern for shows like *Home Improvement* and *Seinfeld* holds firm with *Ellen*, she'll become better known and actually build her audience as the year progresses.

However, professional success aside, it will be some time before Ellen settles into a comfortable place image-wise. For while she may wear the dark glasses, she's not the kind of person who will change the way she lives. Her attitude about the fallout from the tabloids continues to be that people will either like the show and watch it, or not; what she does in her private life should have no bearing on that, and she's probably right. Despite spitting at a baseball game while screeching the national anthem, and despite her various marital contretemps as well as tawdry revelations about her private life, Roseanne Arnold never fell from the top of the ratings.

What, then, can we expect from Ellen during the months when she isn't working on her TV series (usually from March through July, with breaks of two or three weeks scattered in between)?

She wants to do specials that explore other facets of comedy, for both cable and ABC. She's never given that up, even when she started doing sitcoms: she has appeared on *Comedy Takes a Stand, Six Comics in Search of a Generation,* and *One-Night Stand: Command Performance,* all in 1992, and on *Komedy All Stars* in 1993. On June 26 she hosted *The VH-1 Honors,* a live broadcast from Los Angeles which allowed her to work with performers like Stevie Wonder, Michael Bolton, Garth Brooks, Al Green, Melissa Etheridge, and others, including the singer who used to be known as Prince ("I'm going to walk right up to Prince and ask him how to pronounce his new name," she promised. "Bet on it.") She did a terrific job, noting after the opening number, "I could've sworn that Faye Dunaway was s'posed to be singing with them" (referring to the actress's abrupt dismissal from the Los Angeles cast of the musical *Sunset Boulevard*), then pointing out, "I'm not getting an honor. I'm getting nothing at all. But it's an honor to be here."

She would like to do more movies, though that wouldn't take much. Ellen's extremely proud of the Canadian-made documentary, the puckishly named *Wisecracks* (1992), directed by Gail Singer and shot in comedy clubs in the United States, Canada, and England over a three-year period.

A look at the world of female stand-ups past and present and the problems they face, *Wisecracks* stars Ellen along with Paula Poundstone, Whoopi Goldberg, Joy Behar, Pam Stone, Kim Wayans, Maxine Lapidus, Phyllis Diller, and others. Though the documentary is funny and illuminating, *Newsweek* was correct when it described the film as seemingly "illuminated less by sparks of wit than by flashes of anger." (Then again, the anger is justifiable. As Carrie Snow says in the film, women are judged way differently than are men. Club owners "look at you twice: once to see your tits, and once to see what you do.") The magazine did single out Ellen for praise, though, saying that she was one of the few stand-ups who didn't "seem to have the weight of Western Civilization on their shoulders."

And yes: The critic was a man.

To date, Ellen's only nonstand-up movie role has been as "the Coach" (the character didn't even have a name) in the 1993 megaflop film *The Coneheads*. She says that what she doesn't like about making movies is that "there's so much waiting around." But she hopes to do more of them, perhaps even playing some serious parts.

Something else she'd like to do is to regularly get back on the road and do stand-up. It remains her first love, and she doesn't want to lose the comedic edge she first developed there. As Tim Allen says, "Going on the road—you know, that's where it all started. This is where the character came from, and it's this energy that powers the show."

In fact, no sooner had production of the first season's episodes wrapped in May than Ellen did a select number of engagements in Texas, Florida, and several other states, including New York, where her appearance at the venerable Town Hall Theater on June 11 was a key part of the tri-state Toyota Comedy Festival, which lasted eleven days and encompassed seventy-five events.

The Town Hall show may have been the most triumphant of Ellen's career. She sold out the nearly two-thousand-seat house, and when she pulled up in front of the theater in a stretch limousine, dozens of fans crowded around Ellen to get her autograph or pose for pictures with her. She stood in the street and gladly obliged everyone, with unflagging good humor, despite her manager's obvious discomfort at how long it was taking to do so.

Inside, Ellen took the stage and waited while latecomers entered: "Hurry up, hurry up," she teased them. "Run, run, run."

When everyone was settled in, Ellen made the dramatic announcement that she was giving up stand-up to write poetry, then commenced to read the wonderfully awful "Oh How I Wish I Were a Bird." She said that some of the other poems she'd written include "What's There to Smile About?" and "What's the Use, We're All Going to Die?"

After this, Ellen proceeded to run through her classic bits: being sold to the Iroquois, shooting deer, peanuts and club soda on the plane, the mating eagles, the Phone Call to God, and others.

She also managed to cut herself off at the knees at one point regarding her claim that she only works clean: She said that whenever she's flying and hears a strange noise on the plane, her reaction isn't a silent prayer but a loud "Fuck shit damn hell!"

When the ninety-minute performance was over, and a few audience members hurried out to beat the rush, Ellen thanked everyone for the "standing and walking ovation." Fans started shouting for an encore, calling out favorite bits that they wanted to hear, and Ellen was happy to oblige, joking that she should do what Diana Ross does: start the routine, then hold out the microphone and let the audience finish.

However, the fact that one person's superstar is another's unknown was also hammered home at the New York gig: Fans calling the box office for information about her performance learned that

Town Hall was proud to be presenting "Helen DeGeneres."

Ellen says that she had just one stipulation for the new round of concerts and for any she may undertake in the future.

"I only want to work in theaters now," she says. "The environment is so much better for a comic. Everyone's facing in the same direction. You can build the act to a nice strong finish, and you don't have to worry that you're competing with someone in the audience who's drunk."

The shows were sellouts, audiences were wildly enthusiastic, and just before going onstage in one theater she joked, "Boy, they must really like me. Or—hey, did someone forget to take Toni Braxton's name off the marquee?"

The only downside to the tour came in Buffalo, New York, when a trio of tabloid reporters settled into Ellen's hotel to try and catch her doing something rude or lewd. Tipped off to their presence, Ellen's manager quietly had her change hotels.

Ellen was only able to do a short tour this time out so that she could do the VH-1 show and begin the process of interviewing writers and actors for the new season of *Ellen*.

As of this writing, only twenty-six-year-old Joely Fisher—offspring of Connie Stevens and Eddie Fisher—has been cast.

Ellen says that she also has some nonprofessional goals.

She would like to be a mother, she says, but she

really, really *doesn't* want to have to give birth. She equates it to wanting appliances, though she doesn't necessarily want to have to "pass" them, so to speak. Ellen admits, though, that the biggest drawback to having a baby is that "I just don't want to get the same looks I give people" when they bring noisy babies on a plane.

Another goal is to try and find a way to help those who are less fortunate.

"In my day-to-day life I try to be a good person. I love kids. I love animals. It's mean grownups I have a problem with. There is so much hate in this world.

"I cry at least three times a week from stuff that's going on in the world," she says. "Hell, I cry at those sweepstakes commercials, when they go to someone's house and tell them they're millionaires. I love stuff like that. I cry all the time in L.A. Driving around, seeing women on corners with cardboard signs and babies. I give them money, but it's like putting a Band-Aid on cancer."

On the top of her list of personal goals is making her twenty-year class reunion. She missed her tenth reunion in 1986 because she was on the road and couldn't break the engagements but says, "It would be fun to come back" for the next one.

She would also like to go back to Texas or somewhere else in the Southwest, she says, and perhaps buy some land in the area, a ranch or a farm. Despite the fact that she has joked about Atlanta being somewhat unexciting, she likes the fact that in small towns, people will "wave when you pass them in a car, even if you don't know them. I think the world would really be a better place if they did that everywhere." A place like that would provide her with a haven from the pace, pressure, and press scrutiny in Hollywood.

A place where she can be herself.

(She isn't, however, one of those timorous souls who wants to flee Southern California because of the earthquakes. Though she believes that "maybe Earth is angry with us," she recently told Patricia O'Haire of *The New York Post* that she's kind of blasé about quakes: When they rattle the house at night, she says, "I kinda lay in bed awhile, trying to decide whether [it's] big enough to get up for." Most of the time, the answer is no.)

Tim Allen says that one of the great things about becoming famous in your middle or late thirties, like he did or like Ellen has, is that you aren't totally disoriented by it.

"You already have your friends," he says, "your family or your social structure. None of that is going to change. A lot of the reasons people get excited about being in the public eye—the sycophants and bootlickers—mean nothing to you. You don't want or need new friends, so you're much more discerning about who you let get close to you. As a result, you're much more stable."

Ellen is still the individualist she was just out of high school (albeit a much wealthier one), and she cherishes the part of her life that isn't show business. She says that one of her own role models is Jay

Leno. "Jay doesn't take this so seriously," she told reporter James Brady. "If it all ended tomorrow, he'd go home and work on his motorcycle."

If it all ended tomorrow for Ellen, she'd still have her friends and family, and she'd still have her talent.

But it won't all end tomorrow. There will be detours and surprises, unexpected challenges and disappointments along the way, but she's too smart and too funny, too resilient and too individualistic for anything to stop her.

And, most important, she always keeps that precious sense of humor about her.

"Just because I'm a comedian doesn't mean I'm always cracking jokes, that I'm always funny," she says. "If anything, I'm too serious, I think."

Well, she is—but only in private. Give her an audience of even one, and she can't resist the witty observation or clever turn of phrase.

As she summed up her life after finishing one of her recent tour engagements, "I've been up and I've been down, and up is better. Unless you're sleeping, in which case down is better. Especially goose down."

That's pure "DeGenerese" for you.

She may be bigger than ever, with clout to spare, but Ellen's still Ellen, as quick and funny as she ever was.